How to Use This Book

CliffsNotes Adams' *The Education of Henry Adams* supplements the original work, giving you background information about the author, an introduction to the novel, a graphical character map, critical commentaries, expanded glossaries, and a comprehensive index. CliffsNotes Review tests your comprehension of the original text and reinforces learning with questions and answers, practice projects, and more. For further information on Henry Adams and *The Education of Henry Adams*, check out the CliffsNotes Resource Center.

CliffsNotes provides the following icons to highlight essential elements of particular interest:

Reveals the underlying themes in the work.

Helps you to more easily relate to or discover the depth of a character.

Uncovers elements such as setting, atmosphere, mystery, passion, violence, irony, symbolism, tragedy, foreshadowing, and satire.

Enables you to appreciate the nuances of words and phrases.

Don't Miss Our Web Site

Discover classic literature as well as modern-day treasures by visiting the CliffsNotes Web site at www.cliffsnotes.com. You can obtain a quick download of a CliffsNotes title, purchase a title in print form, browse our catalog, or view online samples.

You'll also find interactive tools that are fun and informative, links to interesting Web sites, tips, articles, and additional resources to help you, not only for literature, but for test prep, finance, careers, computers, and the Internet too. See you at www.cliffsnotes.com!

LIFE AND BACKGROUND OF THE AUTHOR

Personal Background

Henry Brooks Adams was born in Boston, Massachusetts on February 16, 1838, the fourth of seven children of Charles Francis Adams and Abigail Brooks Adams. Henry's distinguished family included a great-grandfather, John Adams (1735–1826), who was the second President of the United States, as well as a grandfather, John Quincy Adams (1767–1848), the sixth President of the United States. Henry's boyhood memories included pleasant summers spent at Quincy, the residence of his paternal grandparents located seven miles south of Boston. A nearly fatal bout of scarlet fever shortly before his fourth birthday may have accounted for Adams's diminished physical stature (barely five feet three inches tall as an adult). A trip to Maryland, Virginia and Washington, D. C. with his father in 1850 exposed Henry to slavery and left a lasting impression; he and his family strongly opposed the institution. His formal childhood schooling was at the private Latin School of E. S. Dixwell in Boston where he was graduated in June 1854. On August 31 of that year, he began his collegiate studies at Harvard.

Henry was only an average student at Harvard but did contribute to the *Harvard Magazine* and was Class Orator for graduation. Throughout his life, Adams was critical of formal education; even Harvard could not escape his scorn. Following graduation in 1858, Henry sailed with several friends for the "Grand Tour" of Europe, a tradition that some of the privileged young men of the day enjoyed. Adams's specific plan was to study civil law in Berlin. Finding his German inadequate, he enrolled in a German secondary school. He spent most of 1859–1860 seeing Europe, significantly beginning his writing career by publishing travel letters in the Boston *Daily Courier*. Returning home in October 1860, Henry served in Washington as private secretary to his father, a member of Congress. He was also Washington correspondent for the Boston *Daily Advertiser* during this volatile period, just before the beginning of the Civil War.

Henry continued as private secretary to his father during Charles Francis Adams's tenure as Minister to England (1861–1868); until January 1862, he was also the secret London correspondent of the New York *Times*, a situation that nearly caused him and his father considerable embarrassment (see Chapter VIII of the Critical Commentaries). The American Civil War years (1861–1865) were especially intriguing because his father's work dealt with pro-Confederacy interests and successfully tried to keep England neutral.

Returning to the States in July 1868, Henry concentrated on a career as a freelance political journalist in Washington. He published extensively in journals during this period and earned a reputation as a reformer, especially in articles dealing with American finance and the New York gold conspiracy. While vacationing in Europe in the summer of 1870, he learned that his beloved sister Louisa had been in a cab accident near her home in Italy. He rushed to her side, but she died of tetanus a few days later. Despondent, Henry briefly sought solace in a monastery in England. He received a letter from the president of Harvard offering a position as assistant professor of history and editor of the prestigious *North American Review*. With personal reluctance but overwhelming encouragement of family and friends, he accepted.

At Harvard, he gained a reputation as an effective, innovative teacher and an unorthodox, iconoclastic, sometimes-dictatorial editor. He was an American pioneer in the use of the seminar system, evaluations by students, and the importance of student journals. He introduced graduate studies in history at Harvard and promoted the study of American history.

On June 27, 1872, Henry married Marian "Clover" Hooper of Boston. The couple spent the next academic year on an extended honeymoon in Europe and Egypt. He resigned from Harvard in 1877, moving to Washington to edit the papers of Thomas Jefferson's Secretary of the Treasury, Albert Gallatin. This precipitated a period of extensive publishing that included *The Life of Albert Gallatin* (1879); two novels (*Democracy*, published anonymously in 1880, and *Esther*, published under the pseudonym "Frances Snow Compton," in 1884); a critical biography of the southern statesman John Randolph (1882); and, most important, the *History of the United States of America during the Administrations of Thomas Jefferson and James Madison* (1889–1891), in nine volumes.

On December 6, 1885, Henry's wife, Marian, committed suicide after a long period of depression, a disease that ran in her family. The event was especially traumatic for Adams and the principal reason for his leaving twenty years of his life (1872–1892) out of his most famous work, *The Education of Henry Adams* (published in 1907). He sometimes referred to the rest of his life as "posthumous," but some of his best work was completed after his wife's tragic death.

After Adams's wife's suicide, his friends became even more important to him. He traveled the South Seas and visited Japan with the artist

John La Farge and was especially close to geologist Clarence King and statesman John Hay. Elizabeth Cameron, married to a Senator from Pennsylvania, became his emotional confidante in an apparently platonic relationship.

Henry continued his interest in politics, explored a scientific approach to history, studied medieval philosophy and architecture, and wrote extensively. The Panic of 1893 drew him into the controversy over the gold standard: The question was whether international trade and American currency should be based on gold only or on both gold and silver, which would expand the economy and cheapen the currency. Henry supported the backers of silver and feared a new ruling class of gold capitalists (whom he called *gold-bugs*). He also advocated independence for Cuba. Remarkable advances in science caused him to wonder if scientific method could be successfully applied to the study of history. This is considered in detail in the *Education* and resulted in Adams's "Dynamic Theory of History." An intense interest in medieval philosophy and architecture led to the writing of *Mont-Saint-Michel and Chartres*, printed privately in 1904. He thought of this and the *Education* as companion pieces.

Henry Adams was partially paralyzed by a stroke in 1912 and spent most of his remaining years traveling, resting, receiving dignitaries, and quietly socializing at his home at 1603 H Street in Washington. He died on March 27, 1918 and was buried beside his wife at Rock Creek Cemetery in Washington, D. C. The first trade publication of his *Education* came out later that year and was an immediate best-seller. In 1919, Adams was posthumously awarded the Pulitzer Prize for *The Education of Henry Adams*. In 1999, Modern Library listed the *Education* as the best nonfiction book, written in English, of the twentieth century.

Selected Writings and Reputation

Among Henry Adams's many publications, in addition to the *Education*, four are especially representative: the novel *Democracy*, the biography of *John Randolph*, the *History of the United States of America during the Administrations of Thomas Jefferson and James Madison*, and the *Mont-Saint-Michel and Chartres*. Each illustrates a different aspect of Adams's intellect and contributes to his reputation as a writer of diverse talents and interests.

Democracy An American Novel was printed anonymously in the United States and England in 1880 and was an immediate popular success. With the viewpoint of an insider, Adams quickly shows, through an inquiring but initially naïve female protagonist, that the title is ironic as he exposes the political and personal corruption of Washington. The prototype of this corruption is the fictional Silas P. Ratcliffe, a scoundrel devoted to power rather than principle. The President of the United States, nicknamed "Old Granite" because he formerly worked in a quarry, represents the lowest common denominator of the people who elected him. Somewhat reminiscent of Adams's opinion of President Grant, Old Granite is incapable of coping with the dastardly but brilliant Ratcliffe or any of the complexities of office. Despite its commercial success, the novel has never received much critical acclaim. For Adams, it was a diversion, an entertaining outlet for his wit as well as some of the frustrations left over from his days as a reform journalist. In 1885, he presented the copyright to the National Civil Service Reform League. A 1925 printing was the first to name Henry Adams as author.

In late March or early April 1881 (despite Henry's lack of sympathy for Southerners and, specifically, for John Randolph), John T. Morse, Jr., the editor of the "American Statesmen" series, invited Adams to take on the project of writing the biography of the Virginia orator and politician. Adams pursued the assignment with vigor, producing what Ernest Samuels in *The Middle Years* refers to as one of Henry's "portraits in acid." Randolph was a member of the House of Representatives at the age of twenty-six (1799), during the John Adams administration (1797–1801), and a United States Senator during John Quincy Adams's administration (1825–1829); he was a leading political opponent of Henry's great-grandfather as well as his grandfather. Randolph strongly advocated the States' Rights position, supporting the autonomy of individual states and limiting the strength of the federal government, including the Supreme Court. He even converted John Quincy Adams's Vice President, John C. Calhoun, to the States' Rights cause; because of its impact on slavery, the States' Rights issue would remain a major factor leading up to the Civil War. Published in 1882, the biography of Randolph offers some of Henry's liveliest writing; nevertheless, the consensus is that Henry's passion is too obviously biased in favor of the Adams family.

Adams expected his nine-volume *History of the United States of America during the Administrations of Thomas Jefferson and James Madison* (1889–1891) to be his crowning achievement. He tried to make the work as accessible as possible by using simple language, many primary sources, and a format that would be easy to read. While historians have always respected the work, Adams was disappointed that it was not a popular success, perhaps overestimating the public's enthusiasm for a history of this length. The tone is often abrasive, as it is in the *John Randolph*; Adams is quick to criticize Jefferson and Madison, the former for vacillation concerning the Constitutional problems with the Louisiana Purchase; the latter for his conduct of the War of 1812. Of the two, Adams admires and identifies more with Jefferson, whom he justifiably sees as a fellow intellectual and a man of taste, despite his being a Virginian.

Mont-Saint-Michel and Chartres (1904) is a historical, philosophical consideration of thirteenth-century Christianity as symbolized by the architecture and icons of two famous French cathedrals built during that period. It is also an invitation to visit the churches (someday, perhaps, in person) and the era (in your imagination). Chartres is of primary interest. In it Adams sees the embodiment of a kind of unity and purpose now lost. Despite his enthusiasm for scientific method, Adams is nostalgic for the simple clarity of the past. The point of view is admittedly subjective; Adams creates an "uncle" who is part mentor, part tour guide, to a younger generation. Within that context, the book is a timeless classic. As Ferman Bishop writes, "[This work] retains all of its power to evoke the spirit of the Middle Ages. More than any other book, it captures the feeling of the Age of Faith."

INTRODUCTION TO THE WORK

Introduction

Sometime after he began writing the *Mont-Saint-Michel and Chartres*, Adams decided to create a companion piece, which became the *Education of Henry Adams*. (For thorough discussions of the inception of the *Education*, and the history of the text, see Jean Gooder's "Note on the Text," Penguin Classics edition and Samuels', *The Major Phase*.) The work was completed in 1906 and a private edition of one hundred copies was printed late that year but dated by Adams's "Preface" as February 16, 1907. The avowed purpose of the volume was to provide balance for the *Chartres*, which considers medieval philosophy and the unity found in the architecture and icons of the cathedrals. The *Education* deals with the necessary education, scientific method, and modern multiplicity of the early 1900s.

Copies of the book were sent to those discussed in the text, with a request that each strike out anything found objectionable. According to Ernest Samuels, three copies were returned. In a letter dated February 9, 1908, William James, the prominent psychologist and philosopher, and an occasional correspondent with Adams, responded to the work in detail. Although he found the boyhood section "really superlative," he complained that there was a "hodge-podge of world-fact, private fact, philosophy, irony, (with the word 'education' stirred in too much for my appreciation!)." He protests, as many readers have since, that much of the history is merely hinted at, so that the reader is at a loss as to Adams's meaning. Finally, he questions the efficacy of the dynamic theory of history. Perhaps, he concludes, the approach is more suitable to a study of physical existence. No other readers appear to have had the insight or the courage to write so bluntly to Adams.

Charles W. Eliot, the Harvard president who hired Adams as an assistant professor of history in 1870, is treated well in the *Education* but was annoyed by Adams's condemnation of the institution. He returned his copy, but his comments have been lost. In the company of another professor, he later called Adams and the *Education* "[an] overrated man and a much overrated book."

When Adams decided to allow posthumous publication of the book, after his stroke in 1912, he sent a corrected copy to Henry Cabot Lodge, president of the Massachusetts Historical Society (to whom Adams gave the copyright), requesting that Lodge look after the text and supervise the publication. Adams included an "Editor's Preface," ostensibly written by Lodge but actually Adams's brief *apologia* for the work. In it, he states that this is the "author's" sequel to the *Chartres* and quotes the section of Chapter XXIX in which Adams discusses the two projects. There, Adams finds himself at the "abyss of ignorance," which is his term for the starting point of a new theory of history. Adams sees two dominating points of view in the past several hundred years. The first is unity. The time in history that best exemplified the concept of unity, he says, was the period from 1150 to 1250. It was dominated by Christianity and represented by the works of Thomas Aquinas, the icon of the cross, the exemplar of the Virgin, and the architectural symbolism of the cathedral. He feels that he can best explore this unity by examining two cathedrals of the thirteenth century, Mont-Saint-Michel and Chartres. A second concept is twentieth-century multiplicity. This is essential to the new scientific methods that Adams admires even as he expresses concern about them. The *Education* is, he says, the point of relationship from which he can best examine multiplicity. Adams's "Editor's Preface" concedes that Chapter XXIX is preliminary to his theory of history, which he will develop in the closing chapters of the *Education*. The elaborate ruse of the "Editor's Preface" is typical of Adams, who consistently loved complexity and paradox and went to great lengths to make himself a little more mysterious. How much simpler it would have been for him to ask Lodge to write a preface, or for Adams to write a new preface, replacing or supplementing that of February 16, 1907.

The original preface, accompanying the 1907 private printing, provides the ground rules for the literary experiment that the reader finds in the *Education*. This is not so much an autobiography as it is the biography of an education. Adams employs some of the techniques of a novelist when he speaks of Henry Adams in the third person and uses symbols, themes, and metaphors to develop his topic in a sometimes-cryptic way. The first important metaphor, which Adams explains here, is the *manikin*. Adams emphasizes that this book will not be an exercise in ego. The manikin persona simply serves as a three-dimensional geometric figure, according to Adams. Throughout his life, Adams maintained that there was no legitimate place for "I," the "perpendicular pronoun," in respectable writing. In fact, in the *Education*, he makes no pretense of presenting a complete human being that is himself or anyone else. Rather, the figure called Henry Adams is merely a manikin on which the clothing of education is to be draped, outfit after outfit, to demonstrate whether the attire fits or not; that is, whether the education turns out to be useful. The crucial object of study is not the individual, the manikin, but the clothing, which represents various attempts at education. Consistent with this approach, Adams simply skips over twenty of the most important, personally charged years of his life (1872–1892), never directly mentioning his marriage or his wife's suicide. The reader apparently is to assume that this has nothing to do with "education," but Adams uses the term in such a broad sense that this assumption is impossible. Each reader must decide how detrimental the gap is.

Adams tells his readers that any young man seeking education should expect no more from his teacher than the mastery of his tools. Leaning on the scientific approach that he develops in the *Education*, he suggests that the student is merely a mass of energy. The education he seeks is a way to economize that energy. The training by the instructor is a manner of clearing obstacles from the path of the student.

The metaphor of the manikin and the motif of education being draped in the manner of clothing are reminiscent of Thomas Carlyle's *Sartor Resartus*, a significant influence on Adams. That essay, published in the United States in 1836, anticipates the *Education* in its theme that mankind's deepest beliefs have abated and must be replaced by new concepts that fit the times. This is precisely Adams's point in Chapters XXVIII and XXIX when he argues that the height of knowledge is, in fact, the abyss of ignorance. As if to offer a clue, the previous chapter (Chapter XXVII) is titled *Teufelsdröckh*, "devil's dung," the name of the professor in Carlyle's work. In the *Education*, Adams is saying that the unity of the Middle Ages has waned; it must be replaced by a dynamic theory that takes into account the multiplicity of a new age.

A Brief Synopsis

"Probably no child, born in the year, held better cards than he," the narrator says of the birth of Henry Brooks Adams in Boston, Massachusetts, on February 16, 1838. Through a series of impressions, he introduces the reader to Henry's boyhood world. Winters in Boston are filled with restraint, rules, confinement, school, and a sense of order that is thrillingly interrupted by wild snowball fights. Summers at his paternal grandparents' home in nearby Quincy bring freedom, delight, hope, and a close relationship with Grandfather John Quincy Adams, formerly the sixth President of the United States. Henry is a child of privilege; that, as much as anything, shapes the outer direction of his life. But his world is rapidly changing, a theme that will affect Henry's education throughout the book. Social change comes first. A trip to

Maryland, Virginia and Washington D. C., with his father in 1850, introduces Henry to life in the near South, its appealing informality contrasting with the horrors of slavery, which the Adams family is devoted to eradicating even though it will mean Civil War.

The style of the book affects the reader's understanding. The narrator is Henry in his late sixties; he speaks in the third person, treating the younger Henry objectively except for occasional insights into the boy's attitudes. The reader rarely sees Henry's emotions. Adams speaks of the key figure as a manikin and his education as the various costumes draped across it. The reader soon learns that Adams is using the term "education" in an unusual, broad sense. He has little use for formal schooling, including Harvard College where Henry, as told in the book, is an average student but a good writer and speaker, graduating in 1858 as the Class Orator.

During a two-year "Grand Tour" of Europe, Henry makes a lame effort at studying law but finds that his German is inadequate and ends up devoting a term to learning the language in a Berlin prep school. He returns to work as a private secretary to his father, a Congressman, in Washington during the winter of 1860–1861. Having published some travel letters in the Boston *Daily Courier* while in Europe, Henry becomes the part-time Washington correspondent for the Boston *Daily Advertiser* during the winter of political turmoil leading up to the secession of many of the slave states.

Henry continues to serve as his father's private secretary during Charles Francis Adams's tenure as Minister to England (1861–1868). Frail and small (5' 3" tall), perhaps as the result of a nearly fatal bout of scarlet fever as a child, Henry is not a likely warrior and completely misses the American Civil War (1861–1865). Nevertheless, the war years do contribute to Henry's education and are especially intriguing because his father's *Legation* (mission) deals with pro-Confederate sympathies in England, and he successfully struggles to keep Britain officially neutral.

Henry's writing career progresses despite some bumps. He is the secret London correspondent of the New York *Times* for several months even though he knows that exposure would embarrass his father and the American Legation; he resigns only after nearly being discovered. After Henry returns to the States in July 1868, he works as a freelance political journalist in Washington, earning a reputation as a reformer, especially in articles dealing with American finance and the New York gold conspiracy.

The most poignant passage of the book (in Chapter XIX) concerns the death of Henry's sister Louisa. While vacationing in Europe, Henry learns that she has been in a cab accident near her home in Italy. He rushes to her side, but tetanus has already set in; she suffers an excruciating death a few days later. Henry is despondent and seeks solace in a monastery in England. Soon he receives a letter from the president of Harvard, offering a position as assistant professor of history and editor of the prestigious *North American Review.* He accepts the offer.

Despite Adams's self-effacing claims to the contrary, Henry is an effective, innovative teacher and editor. He pioneers the use of the seminar system, advocates the study of American history, introduces graduate studies in history, and encourages student evaluations as well as the keeping of journals. During the summer after his first academic year (1870–1871), he meets Clarence King on a geological expedition in Estes Park; King becomes a lifelong friend.

The *Education* simply skips the next twenty years (1872–1892). Rarely at ease with emotion or personal matters, Adams apparently avoids discussing the period because of his marriage to Marian Hooper (1872) and her suicide on December 6, 1885, which he never even mentions in the book. He does say that his life has been cut in two; in his letters, he refers to the rest of his life as "posthumous." However, some of his best work remains. He is still interested in politics, advocating independence for Cuba and supporting his friend John Hay's "Open Door" policy in China. The *Mont-Saint-Michel and Chartres* (1904) and *The Education of Henry Adams* (1907) are privately published as companion pieces, representing, in turn, the medieval Christian unity of the thirteenth century and the burgeoning modern multiplicity of the age of science. Adams works to develop his complex "Dynamic Theory of History," discussed in detail in Chapters XXXIII and XXXIV of the *Education.* The book ends in 1905, seven years before Adams's partially paralyzing stroke, which leads to his death on March 27, 1918.

List of Characters

Henry Adams   The central figure of the book is especially interested in history, writing, modern science, the Middle Ages, and various aspects of education.

John Quincy Adams The sixth President of the United States is important here as a role model and loving paternal grandfather to Henry.

Louisa Catherine (Johnson) Adams Known affectionately as "The Madam," Henry's grandmother provides a stable center to his summer visits at Quincy.

Charles Francis Adams Professionally, Henry is especially close to his father and serves as his personal secretary in both Washington and London.

Abigail Brown (Brooks) Adams Patient and proper, Henry's mother is from one of the most prestigious families in Boston.

Charles Francis Adams, Jr. This close older brother encourages Henry to become a writer and teams with him in exposing the Gold Conspiracy of 1869.

Louisa Catherine (Adams) Kuhn The death of Henry's beloved older sister from tetanus, following a cab accident near her home in Italy, is one of the most poignant moments in the *Education.*

John Hay Secretary of State from 1898 to his death in 1905, Hay is one of Henry's closest friends; the two build houses next to each other in Washington.

Clarence King After meeting during a geological expedition to Estes Park in 1871, King and Adams become close friends. Henry judges King to be the brightest and best of their generation and is greatly disturbed by King's tragic end.

Elizabeth Cameron The wife of a U. S. Senator from Pennsylvania, Elizabeth becomes Henry's emotional confidante after his wife, Marian's, suicide, an event not mentioned in the *Education.*

John La Farge An artist well known for his murals and stained glass windows, La Farge travels extensively, most notably to the South Seas, with his friend Henry after Marian's suicide.

The Terrible Conky Daniels A notorious ruffian and leader of the slum "blackguards" in a monumental snowball fight (see Chapter III of the Critical Commentaries), Conky teaches Henry an important lesson about class distinction and chivalry.

William H. Seward Secretary of State during Charles Francis Adams's tenure as Minister to England, Seward impresses Henry with his practicality, opposition to slavery, and support of Henry's father.

Jay Gould His attempt to corner the gold market in September 1869 provides Henry with a wonderful opportunity for reform journalism.

President Ulysses S. Grant Henry finds Grant to be an incompetent, do-nothing president, but Grant's administration allows Henry to advance his reputation as a political journalist.

President Abraham Lincoln Initially unimpressed by the rustic statesman, Henry grows to respect Lincoln's depth and capacity for growth.

Palmerston, Russell, and Gladstone These British politicians broaden Henry's education regarding political morality and practical politics (see Chapter X of the Critical Commentaries).

Sir Charles Lyell A leading English geologist, Lyell helps introduce Henry to Darwinism and the theories of evolution.

Character Map

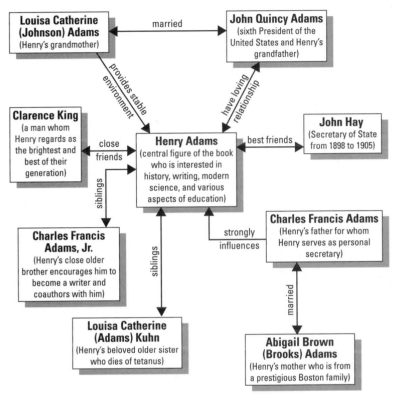

CRITICAL COMMENTARIES

Chapter I (Quincy)

Summary

The book opens with the birth of Henry Adams, "[u]nder the shadow of the Boston State House," in the third residence below Mount Vernon Place on February 16, 1838. Adams briefly refers to his heritage as the great-grandchild of one United States President, John Adams (1735–1826) and the grandson of another, John Quincy Adams (1767–1848). Presenting his early childhood in a series of impressions, he contrasts Boston, where he spent winters, and Quincy, the nearby (seven miles south) summer home and residence of his paternal grandparents. Three events strike the narrator as especially significant: a bout of scarlet fever beginning December 3, 1841; an incident of discipline from the "President" (his name for his paternal grandfather, John Quincy) when the boy was six or seven; and John Quincy's paralyzing stroke on February 21, 1848, which brought the grandfather's death later that year.

Commentary

The Education of Henry Adams is not an autobiography as much as it is the biography of an education. The narrator, in his late sixties, refers to his younger self in the third person. In his "Preface," he introduces the metaphor of a *manikin*, which represents Henry Adams. The various garments draped across the manikin represent his education. The reader will find wit but little passion and less private information in the book. In fact, the narrator will simply skip twenty years (1872–1892) during which Adams was married and his wife committed suicide. In this opening chapter, the reader is introduced to the initial educational impressions of a boy who seems exceptional only by birth.

Literary Device

"Probably no child, born in the year, held better cards than he," Adams writes. Yet the reader is almost immediately told that the world which Adams enters is rapidly changing. It is a world of contrasts. Contrast will prove to be a favorite device of the narrator throughout the book. Here, he sets Boston against Quincy in terms that a child understands. Boston is winter, unity, restraint, rules, confinement, and discipline. Quincy is summer, liberty, diversity, sensual delight, hope, and a touch of outlawry. Quincy is the home of his beloved paternal grandfather, John Quincy, who quietly but forcefully takes six-year-old Henry's hand one morning and marches him to a summer school session that the boy resists, a lesson in responsibility even in Quincy.

Vigor contrasts with illness. Shortly before his fourth birthday, Henry develops scarlet fever and nearly dies. He blames it for his diminished physical stature (barely five feet three inches tall as an adult) and delicate nerves. Shortly after Henry's tenth birthday, his grandfather John Quincy suffers a stroke. His death effectively ends the first chapter of the boy's education. Henry has learned the joy of sights, sounds, and summer play, along with the grim realities of illness and impending death.

Character Insight

The reader begins to suspect that he will not find, here, a traditional definition of "education." Adams lets on that it has little to do with *schooling*. He describes a schoolmaster as "a man employed to tell lies to little boys," foreshadowing his lifelong criticism of formal education, including that offered by a college as prestigious as Harvard.

Glossary

(Here and in subsequent sections, selected names and terms from the book are identified for the reader's convenience.)

troglodytic   like prehistoric people who lived in caves; also, a person who prefers seclusion.

ennui   boredom, as from inactivity.

Cromwellian   revolutionary; after Oliver Cromwell (1599–1658), English political leader.

Cain   Old Testament son of Adam & Eve; he killed his brother Abel (Genesis 4).

imbued   permeated or inspired, as with emotions, ideas, and so on.

Chapter II (Boston)

Summary

The narrator offers a detailed introduction of his father, Charles Francis Adams (1807–1886) and identifies his position on the predominant political issue of the day, slavery. In 1848, the newly formed Free Soil Party nominates Martin Van Buren to run for President and Charles Francis Adams as its Vice Presidential candidate. Henry's impressions of formal religion are as negative as his views toward formal education.

Commentary

It is difficult for any son to evaluate his father objectively, but Henry Adams comes close. He justifiably describes Charles Francis as a man of balanced mind, even temper, and excellent judgment. He lacks John Adams's boldness and John Quincy's imagination and oratorical skills; his intellect and memory are not exceptional. But he is perceptive and clear-headed. He strongly opposes slavery.

The political context needs to be clarified. In 1834, United States Senators Daniel Webster of Massachusetts and Henry Clay of Kentucky had formed the Whig Party from the followers of John Quincy Adams and those opposed to Andrew Jackson. The Whigs were a coalition of western farmers, eastern capitalists, and, most significantly, southern slave owners. Charles Francis Adams could not stand with the slave owners, despite the family's former ties to the Whigs, and bolts the party to join in the formation of a new, anti-slavery party called the Free Soil. The party opposes allowing slavery in new states and territories; it also opposes the Fugitive Slave Law, which allows for the return of slaves captured in free states. Survival of the Union and opposition to slavery will dominate the lives of Charles Francis and Henry for the next twenty years. The narrator calls the Free Soil Party a "chief influence in the education of the boy Henry," affecting his character in formative years and preparing him for the issues, especially the issue of slavery, of the Civil War of 1861–1865.

It is important to notice that, during these years, Henry becomes disillusioned with formal religion. Initially attending church twice every Sunday, reading his Bible, and memorizing sacred poetry, he eventually comes to the conclusion that religion has no meaning for him. Even the moderate discipline of the Unitarian church is excessive. It especially bothers him that "the most intelligent society, led by the most intelligent clergy," turns its eyes away from the social and political problems of the day. Beyond the age of sixteen, formal religion will have no influence on Henry's education.

The boy continues to find formal education a waste or worse. He has a "passionate hatred of school methods." He is certain that studying at home with his father for an hour a day would surpass whatever the schools offer. Henry maintains that he could do well in life if he could master only four subjects: Mathematics, French, German, and Spanish. With typical self-effacement, Adams claims that he never managed to control any of them, but he was actually fluent in French and German. It is true that his later attempts to form a scientific theory of history suffered from his lack of education in advanced mathematics.

Glossary

State Street   here, the financial district of Boston, with ties to southern pro-slavery interests.

aver   to declare to be true.

woolsack   a cushion stuffed with wool, on which the British Lord Chancellor sits in the House of Lords.

Unitarian   a person who denies the doctrine of the Trinity and the divinity of Jesus, maintaining that God is a single being.

naïf   (French) naïve; unaffectedly, or sometimes foolishly, simple.

desultory   disconnected; passing from one thing to another in an aimless way.

Chapter III (Washington)

Summary

As Henry enters adolescence, he begins to notice the complications of life. The stereotypes of class distinction are less acceptable. A trip to Washington, D. C., alerts him to some of the realities of a slave culture. During a visit to George Washington's home at Mount Vernon, in the slave state of Virginia, he becomes aware of the fact that great men can sometimes be associated with wicked practices. He is further disillusioned by a political deal struck by the Free Soilers but is relieved that his father has nothing to do with it. Despite all of these experiences, he writes that, at the age of sixteen, Henry has "had as yet no education at all."

Commentary

Character Insight

The narrator presents a series of experiences that cause young Henry to question the life of privilege that he has taken for granted. The first is a traditional snowball fight in Boston in which the rich West End kids, mostly students at the Latin School, take on the "blackguards from the slums led by a grisly terror called Conky Daniels." At the age of twelve, it has not yet occurred to Henry that *his* group may not be superior in every way. Not only did his paternal ancestors found the country, but his maternal grandfather (Peter Chardon Brooks, 1767–1849) died the wealthiest man in Boston. In the snowball fight, Henry's side prevails initially; but as the day wears on and the ranks thin, the slum kids attack. Outnumbered, the West Enders make a stand; a few flee. Henry is small and weak but stays because his older brother Charles stays. To their surprise, the "terrible" Conky Daniels honors their courage, salutes them with an oath, and sweeps on to chase the flyers. The "moral taught that blackguards were not so black as they were painted." It occurs to the older narrator that boys from both sides would die equally on the battle fields of Virginia and Maryland in the Civil War a dozen years later.

The narrator again employs contrast effectively as Henry's father takes him to visit (in May 1850) Henry's paternal grandmother, widowed and living in Washington. The trip, by rail and boat, takes Henry through his first slave state, Maryland, and later to another, Virginia, to see George Washington's home at Mount Vernon. The boy is struck by the opposing images of freedom and slavery. In the slave states, the countryside is lush and beautiful. There is an impression, even in the city, of an absence of barriers, a relaxed indolence, an open spirit. This contrasts shockingly with the reality of slavery: "it was a nightmare; a horror; a crime; the sum of all wickedness! Contact made it only more repulsive." He wants to escape, along with the blacks, to free soil. While Mount Vernon itself is lovely, it represents the Virginia white owners' profits from slavery. Henry can't fathom the contradiction. How could the father of his country be associated with such evil? He respectfully tries to fall back on the "simple elementary fact that George Washington stood alone." His education has not prepared him to go beyond that.

A political deal struck by some of the Free Soil Party leaders further disillusions the boy. They negotiate a bargain to support a pro-slavery democrat for the office of Governor of Massachusetts in exchange for democratic support of the Free Soil candidate for United States Senator. This is Henry's "first lesson in practical politics" and a shocking one. His one consolation is that his father will have no part of it.

Despite all of these experiences, the narrator ends the chapter by telling the reader that Henry has not yet received any real education at all. In fact, he says, Henry does not even know where or how to begin to look for one. He will next try formal education at one of the most respected colleges in the land—with dubious results.

Glossary

blackguard   scoundrel, villain.

immolation   sacrifice, destruction.

John Marshall   (1755–1835) Chief Justice of the United States Supreme Court (1801–1835), developing the court's role as interpreter of the Constitution.

cant   special words or phrases used by those in a particular occupation.

casuistry   the application of general principles of ethics to specific issues.

conclave   a private or secret meeting.

Chapter IV (Harvard College)

Summary

Henry completes the preparatory course of study at the private Latin School of E. S. Dixwell, Boston, in June of 1854 and begins collegiate studies at Harvard on August 31. The narrator has very little good to say of either experience. Henry becomes acquainted with several Virginians at Harvard, including the son of Robert E. Lee, and claims to like them; but his descriptions of the students reveal a deep prejudice against all Southerners. Henry condemns the course of study at Harvard but blames himself, as well, for his failure to advance in intellect or maturity. Despite efforts at self-effacement, he does seem pleased to be elected Class Orator in a close contest against the class's top scholar (Henry says he himself was an average student) who is, Adams insists, the more popular fellow. Again, Adams tells his readers that education has not yet commenced.

Commentary

The narrator's evaluation of formal education is negative beyond reason. He concludes that Henry's prep school experience was a complete waste of time, an "intolerable bore," and completed with "unqualified joy." Even at his birth, he says, he was too mature for this curriculum! Six years of such study could be surpassed in one; even then, it would have little merit.

Harvard, he claims, is no better. No one takes the school seriously, he reports; it teaches very little and that, poorly. Here, four years could be completed in four months. Harvard College is a "negative force" because it primarily teaches an "ideal of social self-respect." He explains that the wealthy and privileged attend the school only to meet other students from similar backgrounds with whom they will associate the rest of their lives. In even this social sense, Adams claims to miss out: "He made no acquaintance in College which proved to have the smallest use in after life." His association with several Virginians results in an angry, highly prejudiced rant against Southerners: "Strictly, the Southerner had no mind; he had temperament. He was not a scholar; he had no intellectual training; he could not analyze an idea, and he could not even conceive of admitting two." The bias, partly learned from family and partly resulting from a hatred of slavery, would persist throughout Adams's life.

The criticism of Harvard might be easier to dismiss if it came from the openly defiant twenty-year-old Henry who was accumulating an impressive number of disciplinary violations at the college. But the narrator is nearly seventy years old. In the first book of his authoritative three-volume biography (*The Young Henry Adams*), Ernest Samuels discusses Adams's collegiate years. True, Harvard was not at its best when Henry attended. It's somewhat accurate to say that the privileged attended in order to be with each other. Nevertheless, excellent instruction was available. Adams complains of inadequate education in mathematics, for example; but the truth is that he was not very good at math. He was unable to qualify for instruction offered to the top third of the class, and his courses included the basic stuff of algebra, geometry, and trigonometry. Adams further complains that Harvard offered him no introduction to Karl Marx's *Das Kapital*. This is not surprising, however, because the first volume of the work was not published until 1867, nine years after Henry's graduation from Harvard.

Character Insight

Henry does excel at writing and speaking, even at Harvard. He writes several articles for school publications on such topics as appropriate reading lists for college students and the negative aspects of Greek letter societies. His triumph, however, is the Class Oration, delivered on June 25, 1858. It best represents the idealism of the later Adams as he warns of the dangers of capitalism and the vanity of human wishes. Even the older narrator recalls the moment fondly. Still, he claims that Henry as yet knows nothing. After graduating from Harvard, his education has not yet begun.

Glossary

mesure (French) moderation, decorum.

florid flowery, ornate, showy.

delirium tremens a violent reaction to alcohol or alcoholic withdrawal, characterized by sweating, trembling, anxiety, and frightening hallucinations.

desultory disconnected, random, lacking direct relevance.

singular unique, one of a kind.

Chapter V (Berlin)

Summary

Having completed his studies at Harvard, Henry sails for Europe on September 29, 1858 (the *Education* erroneously says it was November) with the intent of studying civil law at a university in Berlin. Adams soon discovers that his knowledge of the German language is inadequate; he abandons the course of law and enrolls at the Friedrichs-Wilhelm-Werdersches Gymnasium where he spends three months attending classes with boys who are about thirteen years old. Formal education in Germany is even worse than in the United States, Adams tells us; but his problems with the language gradually diminish. Berlin is generally a disappointment as a place to live; however, he does enjoy the theater, opera, ballet, and classical music.

Commentary

It was not unusual for a Harvard graduate in the 1850s to take the "Grand Tour" of Europe, indulging in a broadening experience of travel and perhaps some schooling for a year or two. Henry's plans to study Civil Law, which descended from Roman Law and, as Henry knows, was an interest of his great-grandfather, John Adams. Attending his first and, the narrator claims, last lecture, Henry discovers that his German is not nearly up to the task. In a victory of practicality over embarrassment, he enrolls at a local Gymnasium (a middle school or prep school) and spends three months becoming at ease with the language.

By now, it should not surprise the reader that Adams condemns formal education in Germany. He has just cause. The university features "the lecture system in its deadliest form," a professor mumbling from musty outlines as students dutifully take notes. Always eager to suggest an effective digest of course study, Adams avers that more could be learned through books and discussion in one day than the lecture system offers in a month. This is especially significant because it foreshadows Henry's introduction of the seminar system when he later teaches at Harvard.

Although he actually learns something at the Gymnasium, the conditions there are even worse than at the university. The system fills Henry with horror. Training seems arbitrary and stupefying, calling for engagement of only one faculty: memory. Rote drills replace any attempt at thought, let alone reason. In the German mind set, it seems to him, individual thought is subservient to the will of any authority, especially the State.

In addition, the living conditions are horrid. There is no fresh air in the building; children rarely exercise; the food consists of sauerkraut, sausage, and beer. The fact is that Berlin was notorious for its poor sanitation at the time. Open sewers and slum dwellings promoted poor health. As Adams points out, it is one of the least impressive small cities in Europe in the late 1850s. Even the beer is bad, not nearly the quality of Munich's. Only the arts offer Adams respite. Above all, he learns an appreciation for Beethoven. Still, he is more than ready to move on.

Literary Device

A note on Adams's style: He is quick to find fault, tends to exaggerate, loves to startle the reader, and does not always bother with details. But he can write with masterful control. Consistently, he exploits a talent for the facile phrase and parallel structure, especially when he examines paradox, as when he describes a brief stop in London en route to Berlin. Adams comments that, throughout his life, each return to the city will confirm that it "grew smaller as it doubled in size; cheaper as it quadrupled its wealth; less imperial as its empire widened; less dignified as it tried to be civil."

Glossary

captious   fond of catching others in mistakes; quick to find fault.

ingenuous   naïve, without guile.

torpid   dormant, sluggish.

bourgeoisie   (French) the middle class, often regarded as having conventional beliefs, attitudes, and so on.

kinder   (German) children.

Haus-frauen   (German) housewives.

Chapter VI (Rome)

Summary

On April 12, 1859, the semester at the Gymnasium ends; Henry happily leaves Berlin with three friends from Harvard. For the next eighteen months, Henry will pursue "accidental education" traveling through Europe. Although his German continues to improve, an attempt at studying law in Dresden is short-lived. At the end of June, the young men begin a tour of Bavaria, Switzerland, and the Rhine country. Another winter in Berlin seems unbearable. Italy beckons. Early in 1860, Henry begins a "pleasant series of letters," as he calls them in a letter to his brother Charles; they are published in the Boston *Daily Courier*. In April, Henry visits his older sister, Louisa Catherine, who lives in Florence with her husband, Charles Kuhn. Adams ultimately concedes that he has become "a tourist, but a mere tourist, and nothing else."

Commentary

Regarding Henry's education, two important decisions occur between April 1859 and October 1860. The first is that he finally surrenders any pretense of studying law in Germany. Even in Dresden, a city that he much prefers to Berlin, his mind is occupied more with the arts and further improvement of his German. He reads history and novels in German and agrees to engage in conversation in German with his Harvard chum Benjamin Crowninshield. He travels more, eventually arriving in Rome in May 1860. Henry is the first of his family to be granted the luxury of the Grand Tour, and he is concerned that his father may conclude that he is wasting his time. Letters from his brother Charles do scold Henry but encourage him to pursue his talents as a writer.

The second decision follows Charles's advice. Henry begins a series of letters to his brother with the intent that they be published if Charles deems them worthy and can find a newspaper that is interested. The Boston *Daily Courier* of April 30, 1860, carries the first of six letters, all signed "H.B.A.," which will run through July 13. It is not the most prestigious or most widely read newspaper in New England, but it is a start. The letters offer a casual view of current events and stories of human interest from a tourist whose prejudices suggest that he is a child of privilege. When he sees mobs rioting in Sicily, for example, Henry is less concerned with their causes than with their heritage, observing that it is "not good stock" that behaves so crudely. As Ernest Samuels points out in *The Young Henry Adams*, "If these opinions seem painfully superficial, we should remember that they are the complacent insights of a very young man."

By the fall of 1860, it is time to return home. Henry has extended his stay in Europe as long as he can and spent "all the money he dared." With the vague intent of studying law in Massachusetts, he sails for the States.

Glossary

Elbe and Spree   rivers in Germany.

Warte nur! . . . du auch!   (German) from Goethe's "Wanderer's Nightsong" (1780): "Only wait! before long / You too will rest."

conundrum   a puzzling question or problem.

impervious   incapable of being passed through or penetrated.

derisive   showing or provoking contempt or ridicule.

Chapter VII (Treason)

Summary

Henry returns to Quincy in October 1860. On November 6, he casts his vote for the Republican candidate for President of the United States, Abraham Lincoln; that same day, Henry begins the study of law at the office of Judge Horace A. Gray. Again, the effort is short-lived. By the beginning of December, young Adams is in Washington, D. C., where he assumes duties as private secretary to his father, a member of the House of Representatives. Henry will also serve anonymously as the Washington correspondent for the Boston *Daily Advertiser*. The major political issue that winter is the possible secession of the Southern, pro-slavery states, made more likely by the election of Lincoln. On March 20, 1861, the new Secretary of State, William Henry Seward, commissions Henry's father, Charles Francis Adams, Minister to England. Henry is to serve there as the minister's private secretary.

Commentary

The historical setting of what Adams calls "the great secession winter" (in an essay ultimately published by the Massachusetts Historical Society, 1909–1910) is paramount. The Adamses have aligned themselves with the new Republican Party, which took a stand in 1856 to oppose the extension of slavery into the territories or new states. As a moderate Republican, Charles Francis Adams backs William H. Seward in an attempt to preserve the Union and the Constitution through compromise. Above all, Henry's father does not want the North to force Civil War. His position is that the war, if it comes, must be precipitated by the slave-owning states and become *their* act of treason. South Carolina has already announced that it would secede if Lincoln were elected. Senator Charles Sumner leads the radical "Ultras," Republicans who wish to force the issue with the South. Although Sumner has been a longtime friend of the Adams family, dining with them weekly, the friendship ends over this political breach. Lincoln is sworn in on March 4, 1861. On April 12, Confederate troops fire on Fort Sumter in the harbor of Charleston, South Carolina, the first shots of the Civil War.

Although his brother Charles will serve in the war, Henry will be a private secretary to his father, in England, for the duration. Henry's oldest brother, John, will stay home to tend to family business.

Henry's career as a writer develops further as he is appointed Washington correspondent for the Republican Boston *Daily Advertiser*. From December 7, 1860, through February 11, 1861, he publishes a series of unsigned letters supporting Seward's and his father's moderate approach to what he privately recognizes as inevitable secession. The series ends when the newspaper's editor, Charles Hale, appoints himself Washington correspondent. The editor does praise Henry's work, which is noticeably more mature and perceptive than were his letters from Europe. On the delicate issue of secession, for example, Henry's second letter (December 10) attempts to calm his father's constituents by suggesting that "mere temporary secession" would not necessarily mean disunion. The moderate Republicans hope to buy time until Lincoln's inaugural, and Henry's "Letters from Washington" do help. In the end, the moderates achieve their goal: If war must come, let the Confederates start it.

Glossary

prodigal exceedingly or recklessly wasteful; generous to a fault.

lurid vivid in a harsh or shocking way.

Quantula . . . regitur! (Latin) With how little wisdom the world is regulated!

paradox a statement or situation that seems contradictory but may be true.

portentous ominous.

bouffée (French) puff, gust, bombast.

Chapter VIII (Diplomacy)

Summary

Henry and his father arrive at Liverpool on May 13, 1861, the same day that the British Ministry issues a "Proclamation of Neutrality" regarding the war in the United States. Through the editor of the New York *Times*, and without the knowledge of his father, Henry has arranged to be the newspaper's London correspondent. Between June 7, 1861, and January 4, 1862, Henry publishes thirty-two unsigned letters in the daily.

The atmosphere in England startles both Henry and his father. They had expected the English to oppose slavery and support the North; on the contrary, due primarily to financial interests, there is significant support for the Confederacy. On December 16, a supposedly anonymous letter to the Boston *Daily Courier* is identified as Henry's, resulting in considerable difficulty for the young writer.

Commentary

Henry has no business agreeing to serve as London correspondent for the New York *Times*. As Ernest Samuels points out in *The Young Henry Adams*, the State Department clearly prohibits "all communications with the press." Henry might argue that he is not officially an employee of the State Department, serving as a *private* secretary to his father; but he knows that he could put his father in an awkward position and that neither his father nor hostile critics would accept his excuse. Other than contacts at the newspaper, only his brother Charles is in on the secret.

The historical situation is explosive. Instead of finding an England that supports the North and considers the South to be in rebellion, Charles Francis faces avowed neutrality, which puts the South on equal footing. A blockade of Confederate ports concerns cotton processors in England who fear that supplies may be extensively interrupted, causing serious economic hardship. They support recognition of the Confederacy and hope for an early end to the fighting, with the South surviving as an independent nation.

Henry's letters to New York are designed to strengthen his father's position in England; but a separate letter, published in the Boston *Daily Courier* on December 16, nearly destroys his purpose. Henry has visited Manchester in hopes of explaining—and perhaps disarming—the cotton industry's support of the South. His letter on the topic is supposed to be anonymous, but the Boston editor reveals the source. Henry effectively points out that the Cotton Supply Association has experimented with India cotton and may not need materials from the South. Unfortunately, he does not stop there. An incidental paragraph on Manchester social life speaks well of the city but unfavorably of London. "In London," Henry writes, "the guests shift for themselves, and a stranger had better depart at once so soon as he has looked at the family pictures." Manchester hosts provide lovely suppers; in London, a guest is lucky to get a few "thimblefuls of ice cream and hard seed cakes."

After identification, the London journalists have a field day. The *Times* mocks him mercilessly as a "Special Commissioner" to England's "dangerous coast." The *Examiner* recommends softer cakes for the poor boy. Henry is terrified that the London papers may identify him as the author of the letters to the New York *Times*, which would be ruin for him and probably his father. Brother Charles urges him to leave his father's service and carry on a separate fight; but throughout his life, Henry avoids public battles. As soon as he can, he resigns as London correspondent. He needs a more private outlet for his writing talent.

Glossary

Jefferson Davis   (1808–1889) president of the Confederate States of America (1861–1865).

ostracism   rejection or exclusion, as by society.

Quel chien de pays!   (French) What a dog of a country!

Que tu es beau aujourdhui, mon cher!   (French) You're looking fine today, my dear!

débâcle   overwhelming defeat or total failure.

diffidence   lack of confidence in oneself.

Chapter IX (Foes or Friends)

Summary

As the war continues back home, Henry struggles with London's social life. Despite disappointments, he does make the acquaintance of a number of talented writers, most notably Algernon Swinburne. More important is the developing tension between the Legation and British political leaders who favor the South and come close to diplomatic recognition of the Confederacy. One practical crisis involves two warships (the *Florida* and the *Alabama*) that English shipbuilders have produced under contract to Confederacy. Another crisis is primarily diplomatic but even more dangerous as the Prime Minister, Lord Palmerston, attempts to turn an incident at the surrender of New Orleans into an international issue.

Commentary

Character Insight

Although he recognizes the seriousness of his father's role in keeping England from recognizing the Confederacy, Henry *is* a twenty-four-year-old bachelor whose social life is important to him. He feels that he is suffering and, at one point (see Chapter VIII in the Critical Commentaries), makes the ludicrous, self-indulgent observation that his friends in the Union army are "enjoying a much pleasanter life" than he is. Still somewhat superficial and biased, Henry resents the cold shoulder that he receives from the English aristocracy, especially since Henry, frankly, thinks of himself as an aristocrat. On the positive side, English liberals and radical reformers, most of whom abhor slavery, are more congenial. Of special interest to a fledgling writer, Henry becomes acquainted with such talented authors as Robert Browning, John Stuart Mill, Charles Dickens, and Oliver Goldsmith. This year, 1862, he is especially impressed with the young poet Algernon Swinburne. Only a year older than Henry, Swinburne dazzles Adams with his knowledge of literature and his ease of perception; he is a contemporary who is "quite original, wildly eccentric, astonishingly gifted and convulsingly droll." Henry is sincerely humbled.

Of greater concern is his father's struggle to keep the English from diplomatic recognition of the Confederacy. Charles Francis Adams must demonstrate just enough toughness to keep the English in check without going too far and starting another war. Tensions mount when it is discovered that the Confederates have had two cruisers built in England, setting sail as if they were British ships and then being armed from another ship and hoisting the rebel colors at sea.

Even more dangerous is the attitude of the Prime Minister, John Henry Temple, Viscount Palmerston (1784–1865; Prime Minister from 1855–1858 and from 1859–1865). Palmerston appears to be looking for a fight, perhaps hoping for an excuse to recognize the Confederacy. He latches on to an incident at the surrender of New Orleans. There, victorious Union General Benjamin Franklin Butler ordered that any woman who insulted a Yankee soldier should be arrested as a common prostitute. Jefferson Davis, president of the Confederacy, angrily eager to support the honor of Southern womanhood, decreed that, if Butler were ever captured, the General should be hanged as a felon. Recognizing a popular cause, Palmerston rants to the British House of Commons that the Union has disgraced the Anglo-Saxon race! Henry's father calmly stands up to Palmerston, refusing to receive further communication from the Prime Minister except through the apparently levelheaded British Foreign Secretary, Lord Russell. The implication is that diplomatic recognition of the Confederacy would mean war between the United States and Great Britain. Palmerston backs down, but the problems have just begun.

Glossary

remonstrances   protests, complaints, objections.

harrowing   causing mental distress to; tormenting; vexing.

enfant terrible   (French) an unmanageable, mischievous child.

bêtise   (French) blunder.

dyspepsia   indigestion.

Quant à moi, je crois en Dieu!   (French) As for me, I believe in God!

Chose sublime! un Dieu qui croit en Dieu!   What a sublime thing! a God who believes in God!

Chapter X (Political Morality)

Summary

As the war worsens for the Union, the diplomatic situation in London grows more tense. British Foreign Secretary Lord Russell admits that the cruiser *Alabama*, which the Confederacy had built in England, should not have been allowed to set sail until a decision could be made regarding its legality. Increasingly, the affair seems to Henry to be a matter of intent rather than error. He wonders whether *any* politician can be trusted. With the aid of biographical publications, the narrator later examines the events of 1862 concerning a possible British recognition of the Confederacy.

Commentary

Theme

Continuing with the premise of the *education* of Henry Adams, the narrator considers the question of whether the young secretary should simply take for granted the bad faith of anyone involved in politics. Looking at events of 1862 from the vantage point of the early 1900s, with the help of various publications concerning the careers of the principal figures, he discovers that matters were more complicated than he knew at the time.

Recall that, in 1862, it has been less than a century since the United States became a nation, liberating itself from English control. Adams acknowledges Great Britain's financial interests in the Confederacy; but he also strongly suspects a lingering resentment, a desire to diminish the power of a country that declared its independence in 1776. In addition, since the beginning of the Civil War, there has been a concern among the British that should the United States lose the South, they may turn toward Canada for expansion. Additional troops have even been sent to fortify British-Canadian garrisons along the border. A further complication is that Napoleon III, emperor (1852–1871) of France, has an interest in taking Mexico and would welcome a weakened United States. Entering the autumn of 1862, England apparently maintains a position of neutrality toward the Civil War. But things are not going well for the Union. Rebel General Robert E. Lee has entered Maryland in early September. It may be that Washington could fall.

Within this context, the question of political trust *is* educational. The South appears to be on the brink of chasing President Lincoln from the Union capital. On September 14, Prime Minister Palmerston writes to the British Foreign Secretary, Lord Russell, and asks, "If this should happen, would it not be time for us to consider whether . . . England and France might not address the contending parties and recommend . . . separation?" Three days later, Russell responds even more strongly: "Whether the Federal army is destroyed or not," he says, the time has come to intervene and recognize the Southern states as a separate nation. Surprisingly, Palmerston proves the more prudent; he urges waiting for a military result before recognition. Other cabinet members support Palmerston. The Union army rallies, driving the rebels out of Maryland. Despite this reversal, William Ewart Gladstone, Chancellor of the Exchequer (and later Prime Minister), on October 7 makes a remarkable speech asserting that Jefferson Davis and the Confederacy "have made an army; they are making, it appears, a navy; and they have made, what is more than either, they have made a nation." Russell calls for a meeting of the Cabinet on October 23, hoping for diplomatic intervention, which would support the Confederacy. On the same day, he assures Minister Adams that the policy of the British government is to "adhere to a strict neutrality" and to allow the confrontation in America to settle itself. Palmerston opposes intervention; impressed by the Union's recent military success, the majority of the Cabinet joins him. Yet another crisis is barely averted.

The effect of all this for the narrator is to conclude that young Henry has learned absolutely nothing by 1862. Henry trusts Russell and judges him to be more prudent than Palmerston, whom he distrusts. His father and others at the Legation may not share Henry's ingenuousness; but even they have no idea, until years later, of the extent to which they are misled. The lesson, the narrator concludes, is that politicians deceive as a matter of practicality. Even the most trusted would say one thing but do another if they saw such deceit as being in their, or their country's, best interests. If the decisions ultimately prove successful, they are statesmen and heroes. If they are wrong, they are liars and cads. It may be a shock to young Henry, but this is all part of practical politics. A crisis is survived in London primarily because the Union has won its military battle in Maryland.

Glossary

indurate to make hard or callous.

Thurlow Weed (1797–1882) publisher of the Albany *Journal*; a leading anti-slavery editor.

abstruse hard to understand.

The Emancipation Proclamation Revealed by Lincoln to his Cabinet on September 22, 1862, and taking effect on January 1, 1863, it frees the slaves in all states and territories at war with the Union.

superfluous excessive, more than is needed.

turpitude depravity, baseness.

Chapter XI
(The Battle of the Rams)

Summary

Throughout most of 1863, the strain of diplomacy continues in London as the war continues in the States. Minister Adams learns that William Laird & Son, shipbuilders in Liverpool, are constructing two ironclad warships for the Confederacy. Adams sends a series of notes of protest to British Foreign Secretary Lord Russell. On September 1, 1863, Russell writes the American Legation to state that he cannot interfere with these vessels in any way. Adams responds in the strongest possible terms on September 5: "It would be superfluous in me to point out to your Lordship that this is war!" Fortunately, Russell has already reconsidered his position; on September 2, he orders the two warships to be detained. Russell seeks an alternative buyer for the vessels.

Commentary

Minister Adams's diplomatic victory in London is the result of bold candor as well as timing. When the war in the States was very much in doubt, the Confederacy contracted for two ironclad warships, which the narrator refers to as battering rams due to their heavy prows and a method of ramming the enemy. During the summer of 1863, however, the Union gains two decisive victories within a few days. On July 4, the Confederate garrisons at Vicksburg, Mississippi, surrender to General Grant after a siege of more than six weeks. The major port between Memphis and New Orleans, Vicksburg is a key to the control of the Mississippi River. Even more important is the Union victory at Gettysburg, in Pennsylvania, where, on July 1–3, General Meade's forces defeat General Lee's, both sides suffering terrible casualties. The North is at an advantage by the end of the summer, and so is Minister Adams.

Character Insight

The narrator points out that Minister Adams especially *likes* Russell. The British Foreign Secretary reminds Henry of his grandfather, the Minister's father, John Quincy Adams. As part of Henry's education, however, he notices that his father never completely *trusts* Russell.

Henry's father is not about to allow England to build more vessels for Jefferson Davis's Navy. He insists that Russell intervene. Russell initially tries to stall for time as he did during the crisis involving the *Alabama*, that time effecting the vessel's escape. Minister Adams correctly assesses the situation and takes the strongest possible stance by stating unequivocally that this means war! Russell has already reconsidered and capitulates. On September 8, he informs Adams that "instructions have been issued which will prevent the departure of the two ironclad vessels from Liverpool." He then negotiates to have the British navy purchase the vessels, with the likely intent of selling them to another European nation. Henry is learning that, as Gladstone says and the narrator quotes to end the chapter, politicians are the "most difficult to comprehend" of all mankind; the reason is that they say and do whatever best serves their cause.

Glossary

fatuity   stupidity, especially complacent stupidity.

idée fixe   (French) a fixed idea, an obsession.

collusion   a secret agreement for fraudulent or illegal purpose; a conspiracy.

vertigo   a whirling sensation causing loss of balance; dizziness.

coercion   an act of restraining or constraining by force of any kind.

animus   a feeling of hostility or hatred.

Chapter XII (Eccentricity) and Chapter XIII (The Perfection of Human Society)

Summary

After devoting several chapters to diplomatic tensions in London, Adams alters the tone to consider British personalities and the social scene. He sees a propensity for eccentricity in the English character and asks whether this is strength or a weakness. It seems to Adams that eccentrics support the Confederacy. Socially, Henry finds no personal improvement. He challenges the veracity of an acquaintance's observation that the London dinner and the English country-house are "the perfection of human society." Henry sees little of merit in London other than the opera, but he does appreciate the people of Yorkshire.

Commentary

Style & Language

The change of tone allows Adams to direct his attention to English character and social life, which continue to upset him. His prejudices are strong throughout the book, and he does not hesitate to stereotype entire nations. His wit tends toward paradox. Early in Chapter XII, he states that the "English mind was one-sided, eccentric, systematically unsystematic and logically illogical. The less one knew of it the better." This echoes an even harsher observation in the previous chapter, where he contends that the "British mind is the slowest of all minds," as evidenced by the time it takes for the significance of victories at Vicksburg and Gettysburg to sink in. The old-world view of Americans, according to Adams, is equally stereotyped; Europeans think of Yanks as having no mind at all. Instead of brains, they possess economic calculating machines.

Theme

Another Adams absolute soon follows: that the greatest defect among the English is the enormous waste caused by eccentricity. London intellectuals, especially, are literally the opposite of concentric; they are off balance, seldom centered in the same spot on any two issues. They take delight in being odd or unconventional. It seems a compliment at an English club or dinner table to say, "So-and-So is 'quite mad,'" as if being deranged were indicative of greater genius.

With his penchant for being contrary, Adams challenges this point of view. He poses the question of whether eccentricity is strength or a weakness. Adams feels that many Americans, especially Bostonians, are overly impressed with the English and falsely see eccentricity as a sign of intellectual vigor or even courage. Eccentric English adore the non-conformity of rebellion, most particularly that of the South because it represents revolt against the economic dullards of the Union who had the audacity to cast off British leadership in 1776. Adams maintains that eccentricity is weakness because it is ineffective. It does not get the job done, as evidenced by the failure of the Confederacy and the English eccentrics' bungling attempts to aid the South. Eccentrics also tend to underestimate opponents, especially levelheaded New Englanders. The events of 1863, the battles of the Civil War, as well as diplomacy in England, prove his point: "The sum of these experiences . . . left the conviction that eccentricity was weakness. The young American who should adopt English thought was lost."

Socially, Adams is disappointed to the point of resentment. The official assistant secretary of the Legation, Benjamin Moran, mentions Henry frequently in his diary of the period, suggesting that young Adams strikes a pose of disdain only because he is not accepted: "He was there [at a reception] pretending that he disliked it and yet asking to be presented to everybody of note." This is consistent with the tone of the *Education,* in which Adams first yearns for a place among the aristocrats and then, not receiving it, says that the "greatest social event gave not half the pleasure" that he could purchase for ten shillings at the opera. When John Lothrop Motley, a historian and later Minister to England, refers to the London dinner and English country-house as "the perfection of human society," Adams sets off on a rant of condemnation toward the English. They would not know a good dinner if they could find one in London and would not know how to order one anywhere. Conversation is eccentric, and any woman who dresses well must be "either an American or 'fast' [of loose morals]." He does like the folk of Yorkshire for their independence and plain good sense. As for the rest of his social experience, he concludes that it adds nothing to the shifting search for an education that he never finds in England.

Glossary

obtuse not sharp or pointed; blunt.

hustings here, a political campaign.

crank informal word for an eccentric person.

sententious expressing much in a few words.

décousu (French) unconnected, disjointed.

toilettes (French) here, dress or costume.

interregnum an interval between successive reigns; a period when a country has no leader.

Patti Adelina Patti (1843–1919), a famous coloratura soprano.

Chapter XIV (Dilettantism)

Summary

President Lincoln's re-election in November 1864 confirms the strength of the Union as well as the firm position of the American Ministry in England. In order to improve the health of some of the Adams family, physicians recommend that they spend the winter of 1864–1865 in Italy; Henry serves as their escort for a visit of about six months. The Civil War ends on April 9, 1865, when General Lee surrenders to General Grant at Appomattox Court House in Virginia. On April 14, John Wilkes Booth shoots President Lincoln, who is attending a play at Ford's Theatre in Washington, D. C.; the President dies the next morning. The tourists remain in Italy for the season. Concerned with the Reconstruction and facing a hostile Senate, President Andrew Johnson decides to leave the London Ministry as it is and concentrate on other matters. After his return to England, Henry wonders about a future career and dabbles in the arts.

Commentary

Adams barely mentions the end of the Civil War and spends less than half a page on the death of Lincoln. The first topic was of more interest to him in its earlier progress; the second was, he suggests, of little educational value at all.

Character Insight

Initially, the cursory treatment of the death of Lincoln seems especially odd. Keep in mind that Henry is half a world away from Washington and has not been in the States since the beginning of the war. The one time that he saw Lincoln (Chapter VII), at the Inaugural Ball in 1861, he was not favorably impressed. If Lincoln showed any sign of greatness, Henry missed it. Adams saw "a long, awkward figure," plain, apparently absent-minded, seemingly concerned only about some white kid gloves. It bothered Henry that the new President showed "the same painful sense of becoming educated and of needing education" that Henry possessed: "[N]o man living needed so much education as the new President but . . . all the education he could get would not be enough." (106) Lincoln was a frontiersman, rough-hewn, not at all the aristocratic, sophisticated type of leader that Henry had been raised to respect. It does not yet occur to young Henry that Lincoln might turn his need for education into an asset, continually growing in office. Adams later realizes that his negative assessment was incorrect, but Lincoln is never a man with whom he can identify. Henry does briefly contemplate the assassination, but the narrator of the *Education* rarely shows passion about emotional matters. All things considered, it is not so surprising that he shows none here.

Such education as he has achieved has eliminated two possible careers for Henry. His father agrees that the young man is not cut out to be a lawyer. As for diplomacy, Henry feels that nothing could ever match the intensity and excitement of his time in London during the Civil War. Writing seems to be the one remaining profession for him— or perhaps editing for the press. However, his experience with the rough and tumble realities of newspaper work has been disillusioning. He will have to wait to see what his return to the States brings.

Meanwhile, Henry's pursuit of education causes him to explore the world of art; but he finds that he has neither the talent nor the taste to be anything more than a dilettante, an admittedly superficial amateur. His pursuit of a small drawing, possibly by the Renaissance painter Rafael (Sanzio, 1483–1520), convinces him that even the so-called "experts" often don't know what they are doing. He decides to dabble in art for amusement and pleasure but with no more serious purpose.

Glossary

brevet   a military promotion to higher honorary rank but without higher pay.

Turner   Joseph Mallord William Turner (1775–1851), English painter.

bric-à-brac   small, rare, or artistic objects placed about a room for decoration.

anachronism   anything out of its proper time in history, especially earlier than its time.

deferentially   in a courteous or respectful manner.

Chapter XV (Darwinism)

Summary

Henry becomes increasingly interested in contemporary methods of science, foreshadowing his later attempts to apply scientific method to the study of history. The works of two Englishmen are especially important to Henry at this point in his education. Naturalist Charles Robert Darwin has recently (1859) published his seminal work, *On the Origin of Species*, arguing for a theory of evolution. Geologist Sir Charles Lyell, a friend of Darwin, a frequent visitor to the Legation, and eventually a friend of Henry's, has supported Darwin's theory in his *Antiquity of Man* (1863) and the tenth edition of his *Principles of Geology* (1866). Henry is somewhat skeptical of evolution but influenced by the scientific approach.

Commentary

The significance of Darwin and Lyell in the story of Henry's education is that they are early influences in his burgeoning enthusiasm for scientific method. As Ernest Samuels points out in *The Young Henry Adams*, "It is hard to exaggerate the stir caused by the scientific discoveries of the mid-century." Darwin, especially, was front-page news. Influenced early by Lyell and in turn influencing the geologist's work, Darwin proposes that plants and animals develop from earlier forms through hereditary transmissions of slight differences; a process of natural selection determines which will survive. He proposes that species themselves actually change through evolution. For example, individuals in a given generation may have a variation in their physical makeup that gives them an advantage in their environment. If their food source is in a tree, their toes may allow them to climb slightly better; or their necks or legs may be longer; or they may be able to shake the food loose better. Individuals with these characteristics are more likely to survive and reproduce. In this way, the species may evolve. Darwin's theory of evolution poses a direct threat to fundamentalist interpretations of the Bible—Genesis, for example—and this is news in the 1860s. As one reviewer says of Darwin's work, "Old ladies of both sexes consider it a decidedly dangerous book."

Theme

Lyell also bothers fundamentalists by showing geological evidence of man's development of the use of tools, for example, over a long period of time. Darwin's theories are consistent with Lyell's discoveries, and Lyell follows him in supporting evolution. Both negate the likelihood of a sudden event of Creation. Lyell further maintains that changes in the earth's surface can best be explained by continuing causes—not by primeval geological catastrophes as formerly believed. So both argue that there is a process in the development of the earth and its inhabitants.

Portions of these theories have been refined, reconsidered, and even discarded over time. The importance for Henry Adams is that they start him thinking about history in terms of scientific approach. Could the developmental patterns of a society, for example, be understood in the way that Darwin explains evolution? Could a scientist's method of measuring the gradual augmentation and diffusion of heat or the dissipation of energy apply to historical cycles? Could there be a workable dynamic theory of history? Later in life, and later in the *Education*, Adams attempts to espouse just such a theory.

Glossary

vestige   a trace, mark, or sign of something that once existed but has disappeared.

curates   clergymen.

a posteriori   (Latin) from effect to cause; based on observation rather than theory.

intelligible   clear, comprehensible, understandable.

Pteraspis   the first vertebrate, according to Lyell; a fish, existing 400 million years ago, related to the sturgeon, used by Adams as a symbol of sequence and continuity throughout the *Education*.

audacity   bold courage, daring.

Chapter XVI (The Press)

Summary

On a hot July night in 1868, the Adams family arrives in the States after seven years abroad. Henry is thirty years old. After a few months of relaxation and renewing friendships, he leaves Boston on October 12 to become a freelance journalist in Washington; en route to the nation's capital, he stops off in New York and arranges to do some work for the *Nation* as well as the *Post*. Henry's review of Sir Charles Lyell's latest edition of the *Principles of Geology* appears in the *North American Review*. United States Attorney General William M. Evarts hosts Henry in his home until the young man finds suitable housing. Seward is still Secretary of State but is of little practical help to Henry, an example of a favorite Adams aphorism that may seem odd considering his many advantages: "Every friend in power is a friend lost." Ulysses S. Grant wins the presidential election in November. Henry becomes interested in issues involving governmental control of the economy, especially "greenback" currency.

Commentary

Adams does not allow a great deal of insight into his personal life, but certain matters here bear consideration. First, it is clear throughout the book that Henry is a child of privilege. He has unusually rich advantages; if he rarely recognizes this, perhaps it is because he has never known another life. When he arrives in Washington, he points out that the "first step of course, was the making of acquaintance, and the first acquaintance was naturally the President." He is not being ironic. For Henry, grandson of one President and great-grandson of another, it seems quite natural, of course, that the nation's Attorney General should take him to meet President Andrew Johnson. Nor is Henry strapped for funds, although he mentions having to make a living several times in the *Education*. In his adult life, Adams enjoys an increasing annual income, mostly from family and personal investments, of between $6,000 and $50,000, during a period of negligible taxes when a top professor at Harvard or a reasonably successful businessman may make $4,000. As a beginning assistant professor at Harvard, in 1870, he will earn $2,000 for the school year and spend about $30 per month for room and board. So Adams is more than comfortable whether he works or not. Remember, as Jean Gooder points out, that the *Education* was originally written for close friends, many of whom were significantly wealthier than Adams.

Adams's public personality is of interest. He was a small man, five feet three inches tall and slightly built; but he could be quite aggressive verbally. While he often was charming, he was known as a sardonic debater even in social situations. In London, he was not above challenging a casual observation by a hostess who said that she could always tell Americans on sight. He asked her to identify one American and one Englishman in a group of strangers and delighted in pointing out her errors. An acquaintance in Washington in December 1868, Moorfield Storey, reports in a memoir that Henry is an acerbic young man in a social setting, "laying down the law with a certain assumption;" in private, Adams was usually pleasant and friendly.

The issue of most interest to Henry in the late fall of 1868 is the constitutionality of the wartime greenback currency. For purposes of expediency during the war, the federal government issued paper money, which was not supported by gold, by passing the Legal Tender Act. Two cases come before the United States Supreme Court in early December 1868, challenging the constitutionality of the Act. Being a strict constructionist regarding the Constitution, and a supporter of "hard" money (backed by gold) at this point in his life, Henry journalistically takes the side opposed to the government. In an article published in the *Nation* on December 17, Adams argues that the Constitution is based on a "doctrine of limited powers;" regardless of the stress of the times, no government agency has the right to extend those powers. Issuing paper money without gold backing is, he concludes, unconstitutional. Adams even goes out of his way to attack, by name, his recent host, Attorney General Evarts, who has argued that "the safety of the state . . . in times of national peril" supersedes a literal interpretation of the Constitution. The Court initially finds that greenbacks are unconstitutional; soon after, with two new justices appointed by President Grant, it reverses itself and supports greenbacks as legal tender. (For a thorough discussion of the issue, see Ernest Samuels' *The Young Henry Adams*.) Evarts accepts Adams's aggressive attack as part of the business of journalism and continues to befriend the young reformer.

Glossary

flotsam or jetsam   odds and ends.

doctrinaire   a person who dogmatically applies theory regardless of practical problems.

filial   suitable to a son or daughter.

Chapter XVII (President Grant)

Summary

Initially optimistic about Grant's first term in office, Henry soon becomes disillusioned. Because of Grant's success during the Civil War, Henry assumes that the new President will at least be an effective administrator, as George Washington was, and have the wisdom to select top men for his Cabinet. The Cabinet announcements are disappointing to Henry because they indicate political inertia rather than reform. Adams prefers limited control for the federal government, a *laissez-faire* policy; but he does hope that Grant will restore power to the Constitution and get rid of "greenback" currency, which is not supported by gold. A visit to the White House is discouraging. Henry sees only a diminishing future for himself in Washington. As a writer, however, he has some success. The British *Edinburgh Review* publishes his "American Finance, 1865–1869" in April, editor Henry Reeve praising it with such enthusiasm that Henry includes the evaluation in a letter to his brother Charles. The *North American Review* carries two of his articles on the political situation in Washington; the *Nation* runs two on inside information, such as "A Peep into Cabinet Windows," in December.

Commentary

As an educational experience, the first Grant administration is a disappointment; as career advancement for Henry, he feels it is even worse. A reform journalist, Henry has high hopes for Grant's leadership. He is disappointed almost immediately. Grant's popularity is based on his achievements as a military leader in the Civil War; considering this, Henry expects the new executive to be at least an able administrator. "Grant represented order," the narrator says; but young Henry hopes for intellectual vitality and strengthening of the Constitution as well. These hopes are dashed with the first Cabinet announcements, which include choices that support the status quo. An example is the unimaginative George S. Boutwell for Secretary of the Treasury. In an area in which Henry has some expertise, he had hoped for the selection of David A. Wells, a man he considers brilliant and sympathetic to Henry's position. Henry still supports the gold standard and also seeks lower tariffs to broaden America's economy; by March, Henry has pretty well given up. As he says to a friend, there is virtually no hope for change. A visit to the White House is not encouraging. He finds Grant to be an "unintellectual . . . pre-intellectual" type, a man in whom only energy counts, a force of nature who may respond well to a fight but is all action and no thought. Henry is sure that Grant is not being ironic when he states, "Venice would be a fine city if it were drained." More important, Grant doesn't seem to care to be bothered with the problems of the government. When accepting the nomination for the Presidency on May 29, 1868, Grant had famously stated, "Let us have Peace." Henry now takes this to mean that the President simply wants to be left alone! Instead of changing bad laws, Grant maintains that they should be enforced so the people will be outraged and change the laws themselves. Rather than taking the lead, Grants seems to prefer to do nothing. His is a policy of drift; and drift, Adams avers, attracts only barnacles. In an intentionally silly interpretation of Darwin, Adams now wonders how Grant could have evolved from Washington.

Henry's writing is more rewarding. After spending the better part of three months on his financial piece for the *Edinburgh Review*, he is pleased that it is well received. The down side is that such articles are still printed anonymously in England so the essay, which is reprinted in American journals, is not widely attributed to the author. Henry is equally pleased with his work in the *North American Review*, advocating civil service reform, among other changes. Henry argues against patronage in the civil service; he wants to see an elite corps of career professionals. Henry's reputation as a writer is on the rise. Still, he is concerned about his career as a reformer in the stagnant political atmosphere of the Grant administration.

Glossary

demimonde   (French) the class of women who have lost social standing due to sexual promiscuity; prostitutes.

abject   of the lowest degree; miserable; wretched.

abet   to incite, sanction, or help, especially in wrongdoing.

a priori   (Latin) from cause to effect; from a generalization to particular instances.

lugubrious   sad or mournful, especially in an exaggerated or ridiculous way.

Chapter XVIII (Free Fight)

Summary

Even in the dormant Grant administration, a young reformer soon has plenty to write about. On September 24, 1869, the price of gold crashes spectacularly, exposing a scheme involving financiers Jay Gould and James Fisk as well as President Grant's own brother-in-law. The Legal Tender Act is still an issue, and Adams is concerned that the Constitution has lost its effectiveness because of emergency measures taken by the Lincoln administration during the Civil War. While they oppose slavery, for example, the Adams men maintain that even the Emancipation Proclamation was actually unconstitutional.

Commentary

Adams often writes in cryptic terms in the *Education*, dropping a name here or an issue there with the assumption that his reader is thoroughly versed in the history of the time. With his initial audience, a close circle of friends, that may have been the case; later readers may need a little explanation.

The Gold Scandal of September 1869 allows Henry and his brother Charles to work as an investigative team. Jay Gould, president of the Erie Railroad and a capitalist known for his financial manipulations—along with his associate, James Fisk—attempts to corner the market in gold during the late summer of Grant's first year in office. The approach is to purchase as much American gold coin and bullion as possible in order to control the price. If successful, the scheme could then effect a monopoly, and the gold would sell at a much higher rate to those whose contracts require them to pay off debts in gold. This would especially impact foreign trade because other countries are reluctant to accept greenbacks. The two bring Grant's brother-in-law, a man named Corbin, into the deal with the expectation that this will dissuade Grant from intervention. On Black Friday, September 24, the price of a gold dollar (1/20 of an ounce) rises as high as $1.65 in paper money. At this point, Grant belatedly orders Secretary of Treasury Boutwell to place on sale $4,000,000 worth of government gold. The price of gold plummets, setting off a panic on Wall Street. Gould somehow knows of the Treasury sale in advance and sells his gold near the top price. Fisk, however, is not informed and is still buying as the price sinks. Although no one can prove that Grant or members of his Cabinet are directly involved in the scheme, Henry feels that the circumstantial evidence is overwhelming. (See Ernest Samuels' *The Young Henry Adams* and Jean Gooder, ed., the Penguin Classics edition of the *Education* for further comments.)

For Henry and Charles, the scandal is, as Henry says in the *Education*, "heaven-sent." Charles investigates corruption in the management of the railroads; Henry pursues the gold conspiracy and even gets an interview with James Fisk. James A. Garfield, who in 1881 will become the twentieth President of the United States (assassinated that year), heads an investigation as chairman of the House Committee on Currency and Banking. He exchanges information with the Adams brothers. For Henry, the result is one of his most highly praised articles, "The New York Gold Conspiracy," in the *Westminster Review* (October 1870). Although he is disappointed that more prestigious publishers refuse the piece, fearing charges of libel, he is delighted that the work is widely distributed in "pirated" versions. Charles's exposé of the railroads is so effective that his life is threatened. He survives, unharmed, to father five children and die at the age of eighty in 1915.

Character Insight

Henry is pleased with the reception of other articles, especially "The Legal Tender Act" in *North American Review* (April 1870), which accuses Congress of "a piece of intolerably impudent political abuse." He argues again against greenbacks and reiterates his belief in *laissez-faire* economics, hoping that the Grant administration will return the government's position to a hands-off policy. In another installment of political assessments called "The Session," in the *North American Review* (July 1870), he calls for Grant to restore the power of the Constitution and the federal government's system of checks and balances. All expectations to the contrary, it has been a productive and rewarding period for Henry.

Glossary

profligate   immoral and shameless.

âme damnée   (French) stooge; a foil or underling.

skein   here, a sequence or series of events.

peremptory   barring further action; final.

putative   considered or deemed such; reputed.

fiat   an order issued by legal authority.

Chapter XIX (Chaos)

Summary

Henry returns to London in May of 1870 expecting a relaxing vacation after submitting his key essays for publication. The peaceful order of his life is turned to chaos when he receives a telegram informing him that his sister Louisa Catherine (Adams) Kuhn (1831–1870) has been thrown from a cab and injured. Tetanus has already set in when he arrives at her home in Italy. After ten days, she dies in convulsions. Having spent the Civil War years in London, Henry has not seen a great deal of death; he is profoundly affected by it. The Franco-Prussian War (1870–1871), beginning that summer, seems to echo the terrible turbulence in his soul.

Commentary

Adams is reluctant to write about his personal life in the *Education* and rarely shows emotion. An exception is the section of this chapter concerning the death his beloved sister, the oldest of the siblings. Allowing the reader into his troubled heart, Adams produces some of the finest writing in the book. He says that his "last lesson—the sum and term of education—began" when he learned of his sister's accident. Henry immediately travels to her home in Italy, a trip of two days; she is already dying of tetanus, an acute infectious disease that can easily be avoided today by way of inoculation. The narrator poignantly observes: "He had passed through thirty years of rather varied experience without having once felt the shell of custom broken. He had never seen nature—only her surface—the sugar-coating that she shows to youth."

This is a different Henry Adams, as a man and a writer. With deep feeling, he contrasts his sister's tragic situation with her strong spirit, which still is as it was during the "careless fun of 1859" when he had visited her: "Hour by hour the muscles grew rigid, while the mind remained bright, until after ten days of fiendish torture she died in convulsions." Entering the body through even a minor wound, tetanus typically causes spasmodic contractions; rigidity of voluntary muscles, especially in the jaw, face and neck; and, if unabated, death. Adams faces the usual clichés regarding death, the "thousand commonplaces of religion and poetry" intended to "veil the horror." None suffices. He observes that death "took features altogether new to him. . . . Nature enjoyed it, played with it, the horror added to her charm, she liked the torture, and smothered her victim with caresses." He is overwhelmed by the contrast between death and the joy of life surrounding the scene, the vitality of friends, the "soft, velvet air, the humor, the courage, the sensual fullness of nature and man." He finds no spiritual ease, concluding, "God might be, as the Church said, a Substance, but he could not be a Person."

Henry seeks stability with friends in the Alps but sees in nature only chaos, anarchy, and purposeless force. The Franco-Prussian War soon imposes a further sense of disorder and ruin. Henry flees to Wenlock Abbey in England, taking refuge in the profound peace of contemplation with the few monks who live there. He then receives a letter from Charles William Eliot, president of Harvard University, inviting him to accept a position as assistant professor of history, coupled with editorship of the *North American Review*. With distinct personal reservations, but the overwhelming encouragement of family and friends, he accepts.

Glossary

rococo   a style of music, architecture or decorative art characterized by profuse and delicate ornamentation, reduced scale, lightness, and grace.

atrophy   a wasting away, especially of body tissue, due to disuse or lack of nutrition.

abate   to make less in amount or degree.

affiches   (French) posters, placards.

tour de force   (French) feat of strength; an unusually skilled creation or performance.

Chapter XX (Failure)

Summary

Henry Adams serves Harvard as a history professor and editor of the prestigious *North American Review* from 1870 to 1877, taking a leave of absence during the 1872–1873 academic year to travel Europe with his new bride. Only the first year is discussed in the *Education.* He initially lectures to three classes per week but is free to address any topic he wishes within the years 800 to 1649. Henry immediately feels that he is in over his head. He tells a friend that he has returned to college not so much to teach as to learn. He claims that he is barely able to stay a day ahead of his students; he is not an expert in the field, although he does have specific pockets of expertise such as medieval architecture. Partly out of desperation, Henry experiments with various approaches to teaching. Editing also takes a good deal of his time, and he welcomes a vacation to Wyoming and Colorado when his duties end for the summer of 1871.

Commentary

Adams appears to be overly self-effacing, even disingenuous, about his "failure" as a Harvard professor. In fact, he is quite successful; but it is a success born of necessity and limited by what he sees as an inept system. Henry is exaggerating, but just a little, when he says that he is completely unqualified for the job: Adams is not a trained teacher nor a medieval scholar. He is only barely kidding when he writes to a friend in January 1871 that his students will never be able to check his facts and theories later because he has invented most of them! Nevertheless, he does have a deep interest in his subjects and even more in his students. For all his grousing, he deeply loves interaction with the young scholars. One of Adams's best known statements refers not to politics but to teaching: "A teacher affects eternity; he can never tell where his influence stops. Henry soon decides, however, that he is going to have to affect eternity in some revolutionary ways.

Henry Adams is not the first professor to advocate use of the seminar, graduate studies in history, or student journals. He has seen seminars in Germany and probably discussed the technique with an acquaintance and distant relative, Professor Charles Kendall Adams, who inaugurated a seminar in history at the University of Michigan in 1869 and visited Henry early in 1871. But Adams is a pioneer in their application to American, and especially Harvard, education. Henry is fortunate to have one small honors class (most were much larger), "half a dozen highly intelligent young men," with which to experiment. Saying that he knows no more than his students, and lacking a proper textbook, he drops the lecture format, challenging the students to read what they please within the broad spectrum of this course (from primitive man to the Norman Conquest in 1066) and then compare results. The experiment works; the scholars learn to "chase an idea, like a hare." In class, they discuss and debate. Henry meets students in his own rooms rather than the lecture hall. He wishes that he could attend the meetings of the class with another professor, each of them taking contradictory positions on issues. But he also sees value in simply holding his tongue and allowing the class to come to its own conclusions. He wants student evaluations of courses, professors, and the students' collegiate experience. He recommends that the students keep diaries or journals. He complains that most classes are too large and financial interests given inordinate weight: "No man can instruct more than half a dozen students at once. The whole problem of education is one of its cost in money," Eventually, Henry applies his seminar approach to a graduate program in history at Harvard. If some of this sounds familiar to contemporary American students or educators, they can thank Henry Adams.

Although he claims to have no time for writing, Henry publishes at least twenty-two reviews and articles (usually unsigned) in the *North American Review* during his tenure as editor. To no one's surprise, he is a rebel and iconoclast as an editor, promising twenty pounds to one writer "if you are abusive enough" and instructing another, "Stand on your head and spit at someone." He thinks of himself as an active collaborator with full powers of revision; others sometimes complain that he is too "dictatorial," as early suffragette Lucretia Mott put it.

At the end of the school year, Henry is exhausted and welcomes an invitation to join the Fortieth Parallel Expedition in a geological survey near Estes Park. There he meets Clarence King, an extraordinary scientist and man who will be one of Henry's closest friends for life.

Glossary

pedagogy   the art or science of teaching; teaching methods.

pedant   here, a narrow-minded teacher who insists on exact adherence to arbitrary rules.

avatar   incarnation of a god or of some quality in a person.

Chapter XXI (Twenty Years After)

Summary and Commentary

This transitional chapter helps Adams to skip more than twenty years of his life during which he married Marian "Clover" Hooper of Boston (on June 27, 1872), taught at Harvard until 1877, published widely, traveled widely, and suffered through his wife's suicide (December 6, 1885). During his year's leave from Harvard (1872–1873), Adams traveled throughout Europe and Egypt with his bride; after her death, John La Farge, a noted artist, former Harvard associate, and devoted friend, accompanied him to Japan and later to Hawaii, Samoa, Tahiti, Fiji, Australia, and Ceylon. Adams's publications during this period included two novels, two biographies, and one of his most important works, the *History of the United States of America during the Administrations of Jefferson and Madison* (in nine volumes). His wife's suicide, following a long depression, was especially traumatic for Adams and the primary reason for eliminating this period (1872–1892) from the book. He does not address the topic directly in the *Education* but writes, "Life had been cut in halves, and the old half had passed away, education and all, leaving no stock to graft on." He sometimes refers to the rest of his life as "posthumous." (Students can find helpful guides to the events of these years in Ernest Samuels, *Henry Adams: The Middle Years,* as well as the second and third volumes of *The Letters of Henry Adams.*)

By the middle of February 1892, Adams is again in Washington. Just before the death of his wife, the Adamses and Mr. and Mrs. John Hay built homes next to each other facing Lafayette Square. Hay, Adams, and Clarence King are inseparable friends, the narrator says; James Donald Cameron and, especially, his young wife, Elizabeth, are also close friends. Adams foreshadows the depression of 1893 through a veiled reference to the collapse (in 1891) of the world's leading banking firm, London's House of Baring, which caused a worldwide recession and led to the depression. Adams was in Samoa at the time: "Even the year before, in 1891, far off in the Pacific, one had met everywhere in the east a sort of stagnation—a creeping paralysis . . . [q]uestions of exchange and silver-production loomed large." This introduces a major topic of the next chapter, in which Adams will re-assess his position on the gold standard. Even though he is still despondent about his wife's death, Adams is drawn to this financial issue. Henry has, he says, "an uneasy distrust of bankers. Even dead men allow themselves a few narrow prejudices."

Glossary

inertia   a tendency to remain in a fixed condition without change; disinclination to move or act.

stentorian   very loud (after the Greek herald in the *Iliad*, with the voice of fifty men).

viscosity   the state or quality of having a cohesive and sticky fluid consistency.

torpor   a state of being dormant or inactive.

A la disposicion de Usted!   (Spanish) At your service!; At your disposal!

Chapter XXII (Chicago)

Summary

The international depression of 1893 draws attention to the issue of the gold standard in the United States. The question is whether international trade should be based on payment of balances in *gold only* or one that includes gold *and* silver, which would involve a fixed ratio of the value of the two metals. Although he still opposes fiat greenbacks, Adams alters his strict support of the gold standard and aligns with the silver backers. A trip to the Chicago World's Fair startles Henry, forcing him to recognize the enormous growth of science, specifically in the field of electricity.

Commentary

The economy captures Henry's attention for personal as well as philosophical reasons. He briefly fears facing bankruptcy at the age of fifty-five, and he questions the wisdom of the gold standard, which places too much power in bankers in Europe as well as the urban eastern portion of the United States.

Theme

As Ernest Samuels points out, speculation and financial expansion in Europe and the United States exceeded realistic limits in the early 1890s, leading to problems with excessively risky loans at The House of Baring in London. Almost immediately, investors begin to sell rather than buy. London capitalists dump American securities on the market, and gold flows out of the States to pay them. The stock market nearly collapses. Many of Henry's friends are among those in desperate financial trouble. As early as December 12, 1890, John Hay writes Adams that "a tornado of falling stocks" has diminished their wealth "by an average of ten million apiece." Henry's close friend Clarence King loses most of his fortune and takes refuge in an asylum. There is a run on banks, depositors insisting on withdrawing their money. Hoarding exacerbates the shortage of currency. More than 300 banks close by July 1893, including several in Kansas City where Henry's brother Charles has extensive interests. The gold reserve at the treasury falls to less than $100,000,000. Returning from a trip to Europe in August, Henry finds panic and despair. He soon discovers that his own conservative investments are not seriously impaired, but he suspects collusion among English capitalists, the Bank of England, the Chancellor of the Exchequer, and the Rothschild banking syndicate throughout Europe—many of his old enemies.

Character Insight

Henry now sides with the backers of silver—mostly Westerners, small businessmen, laborers, debtors, and farmers—who advocate an expanding economy and cheaper currency. He supports the Sherman Silver Purchase Act of 1890, which allows for increase in the coinage of silver. Gold backers (whom Henry calls *gold-bugs*) in the Senate seek its repeal. Despite the support for silver of Henry's friend Senator J. D. Cameron of Pennsylvania, the gold-bug interests are too influential and win the day. The Senate repeals the Silver Purchase Act. During his visit to the Chicago World's Fair, Henry envisions a new ruling class of gold capitalists who will dominate science and technology: "the capitalist system with all its necessary machinery." Henry is no socialist, but he thinks that there is too much power among those who control money.

Glossary

fin-de-siècle   (French) end of century, especially the 1890s.

oblivious   here, unmindful; blithely unaware.

croupier   a person in charge of a gambling table.

jobbery   the carrying on of public or official business dishonestly for personal gain.

naïveté   (French) the quality or state of being unaffected, simple, childlike, credulous.

Chapter XXIII (Silence) and Chapter XXIV (Indian Summer)

Summary

In the aftermath of the depression of 1893, Adams discusses the unfortunate fate of Clarence King, perhaps the man he admires most in his generation. King and Adams visit Cuba in February and March of 1894, enjoying the sights but also noticing an increasing revolutionary spirit opposing the rule of Spain. Adams becomes devoted to the concept of Cuban independence, proposing to Congress a peaceful, diplomatic resolution in an address titled "Recognition of Cuban Independence," delivered on December 21, 1896. Because diplomacy fails, Adams welcomes the Spanish-American War of 1898. Intellectually, he enjoys a kind of "Indian summer," a period of tranquility and reflection preceding his engagement with theories of science and history in the early 1900s.

Commentary

Character Insight

Henry's interest in Cuba is the direct result of his friendship with Clarence King, the geologist whom he met in Estes Park in the summer of 1871 and with whom he shared a close friendship for the rest of King's life. Even at first meeting, Adams valued King among the greatest men he'd known and felt that he had all the qualities that Henry most admired. It is especially disturbing to Henry that King is destroyed in the Panic of 1893. Not only does his dear friend lose most of his fortune, but his mental stability is also rocked, landing him in the Bloomingdale asylum. From there, King writes to Henry in January 1894, proposing a trip to Cuba: "What do you say to taking the island trip with me?" Recognizing King's expertise in the third world, Henry jumps at the chance. Adams visited the island briefly in 1888, but he anticipates seeing the *real* Cuba with King. Henry jokes to a friend, "I expect to find a Carib woman and never reappear among civilized man."

Theme

In addition to the sights, the native dances, and all the local color, the two middle-aged adventurers notice a ferment of political unrest. Traveling companions often comment on Henry's devotion to correspondence, which one can study in the six volumes of his *Letters*. In the South Seas a few years earlier, La Farge noticed that Adams even took along his pen, paper, and writing board while traveling in a canoe in order to dash off a letter. In Cuba, Henry spends the evening writing letters while King mixes with the local population. King hears of a coming rebellion, which grows out of resentment toward subjection to cruel Spanish rule. If anything, the Ten-Year War for Cuban independence, ending in failure in 1878, had just made matters worse; the economy is suffering, and the prison system is notoriously harsh. Adams and King discuss the apparently burgeoning revolution. Henry returns to the States an advocate of Cuban independence. An active revolution does begin on the island in 1895. Adams's speech to Congress in 1896, calling for diplomatic intervention, fails to elicit the desired response. War with Spain seems the only way out.

Thanks to the preparations of Assistant Secretary of the Navy Theodore Roosevelt, the United States is superior to Spain as a sea power; and Americans are itching for a fight. Businessmen would like Spain out of the area. The U.S. battleship *Maine* is sent to the Havana in December 1897, ostensibly to protect United States citizens and property. During the night of February 15, 1898, a horrendous explosion sinks the *Maine*, killing 260. New York newspapers owned by Joseph Pulitzer and William Randolph Hearst (respectively, the *World* and the *Journal*) blame sabotage and call for war, echoing the cry, "Remember the *Maine!*" On April 25, Congress declares war. The conflict is over by July as a Spanish naval squadron is destroyed attempting to cross a blockade in Santiago harbor. Henry hears about the battle by telegram at Kent on July 4, calling the victory "the destruction of the Spanish Armada." Adams's old friend John Hay is Secretary of State. Adams supports Hay's settlement with Spain: independence for Cuba, while Puerto Rico, Guam, and the Philippines are ceded to the United States. In 1969, U.S. Navy research determines that an explosion in a defective boiler caused the explosion that sunk the *Maine*.

Theme

Henry is ready for a new, final phase of intellectual energy. He has been studying the architecture of medieval churches and thinking about the power of Christianity and how it might be compared to the new power released by science. He sees a connection.

Glossary

satiated   filled, satisfied, having had enough or more than enough.

prattle   to speak in a childish way; babble.

debauch   to lead astray morally; to corrupt.

superannuated   old-fashioned or obsolete.

impunity   free from punishment.

embêtement   (French) nuisance, a bother.

Chapter XXV
(The Dynamo and the Virgin)

Summary

Henry is infatuated with the Paris Exposition of 1900, which opens on April 15 and runs through the month of November. He has been studying Gothic architecture since 1895, foreshadowing his historical and philosophical meditation, *Mont-Saint-Michel and Chartres*, privately printed in 1904. During the summer of 1900, he is also reading medieval philosophy. Even with temperatures in the nineties, Henry enjoys this summer in Paris. In July, he writes to Elizabeth Cameron that Thomas Aquinas serves as "liquid air for cooling" his heated blood. Always interested in contrasts and dichotomy, Henry begins to speculate about the medieval strength of Christianity and how it relates to the twentieth-century power generated when mechanical energy produces electricity; this theme will captivate him for the rest of his active intellectual life. In late 1900 or early 1901, he writes a long poem, "Prayer to the Virgin of Chartres," which includes a section titled "Prayer to the Dynamo."

Commentary

Henry approaches both medieval Christianity and modern technology with skepticism, but comes to respect each in its own time. Through his studies of Gothic architecture, with its spires reaching toward the heavens, and medieval philosophy, with its emphasis on God's will, Adams has gained an appreciation for the significance of the Church in the lives of medieval Christians. As a historian, he looks for relevant sequences that tell something about the story of mankind. With one exception, he is disillusioned: "Satisfied that the sequence of man led to nothing and that the sequence of their society could lead no further, while the mere sequence of time was artificial and the sequence of thought was chaos," he turns to the sequence of *force*. By "force," Adams means the power that motivates or attracts spiritual or intellectual lives. As discussed in Chapter XXXIII, this force works with something like a gravitational pull. In medieval times, he sees the Church and, symbolically, the Virgin, the mother of Christ, as providing that motivating, attracting force. As Thomas Aquinas wrote (in *Two Precepts of Charity*) in 1273, "Three things are necessary for the salvation of man: to know what he ought to believe; to know what he ought to desire; and to know what he ought to do." He is to believe in the teachings of Christ; he is to desire service to God and salvation; he is to do as the Church prescribes.

For modern man, Adams asserts, technology, represented symbolically by the dynamo, has replaced the Church. Adams does not necessarily prefer this; as a historian, he simply attempts to describe what is happening. Modern man *believes* in technology; he *desires* what he thinks will be scientific progress; he must *do* what he can to advance with technology. The question of control is undecided by Adams because its answer lies in the future. At one point, decades before the first computer, he even predicts that the time may come when artificial intelligence is so advanced that man will serve machine.

Toward the end of 1900 or the beginning of 1901, Adams expresses the dichotomy in his poem "Prayer to the Virgin of Chartres," which includes the "Prayer to the Dynamo." He sends the first copy to Elizabeth Cameron who has played a key role in Henry's emotional life since his wife's suicide. Their friendship needs mention. Nineteen years his junior, and still married to his good friend Senator James Donald Cameron, she has become his confidante. He often sends her private poems. Elizabeth clearly admires Henry's intellect, maturity, and wisdom. Sometimes they tease, in letters, about rumors of a romance; but the relationship appears to have been platonic.

Theme

The "Prayer to the Virgin" recognizes the force of Christianity in the twelfth and thirteenth centuries, as expressed in the belief in miracles attributed to Our Lady as well as belief in the Madonna's intervention through prayer. The narrative voice is that of Western Man, who journeys back through time to seek guidance from the Virgin. He has lost his innocence along with his belief and finds himself in a materialistic world in which men worship the dynamo. Well into the poem, he offers an example of a modern prayer, "the last / Of the strange prayers Humanity has wailed." This is the "Prayer to the Dynamo." The narrator fears that mankind must master technology or be mastered by it: "Seize, then, the Atom! rack his joints! / Tear out of him his sacred spring! / Grind him to nothing!" At this point, Henry is looking back to medieval belief with some nostalgia. He is a little over-whelmed by the enormous scientific advances of the late nineteenth century, which include, for example, the first small, high-speed com-bustion engine; the automobile; the discovery of X-rays; and the iso-lation of radium by the Curies, all alluded to in this chapter of the *Education*. Soon, Henry will try to use a scientific approach to under-stand the sequence of history. His religious skepticism has turned to admiration for, if not belief in, medieval Christianity and the symbol of the Virgin. Next, he will turn to technology.

Glossary

electric tram   here, the basket or car of an overhead conveyor.

occult   hidden, concealed, secret, esoteric.

parricide   the act of murdering one's parent.

310   It was actually AD 313 when Roman Emperor Constantine the Great converted to Christianity. The Nicene Creed, a confession of Christian faith, was adopted at the first Nicene Council in 325.

folle   (French) mad, insane, out of control.

tortuous   full of twists and turns.

Chapter XXVI (Twilight) and Chapter XXVII (Teufelsdröckh)

Summary

Adams considers the achievements of his friend John Hay, Secretary of State (to Presidents McKinley and then Theodore Roosevelt) from 1898 until his death in 1905. Hay's participation in the Open Door Policy regarding China, the quelling of the Boxer Rebellion, and the planning of the Panama Canal are of particular interest. While Henry does not always agree with Hay, he admires the leadership that his friend gives the country. The contrast between unity and multiplicity takes on added meaning for Henry. He attempts to place the concepts within the Hegelian dialect of contradiction.

Commentary

Writing initially for a circle of relatively close friends, the narrator continues his habit of fleetingly mentioning events as if the reader is thoroughly familiar with them. Here, they have to do with John Hay's tenure as Secretary of State. Under President McKinley, Hay established an Open Door policy (begun in 1899) in China. This was designed to guarantee equal trade opportunities for all interested countries. Adams is concerned that his friend is taking too great a risk because of China's defensive posture toward its traditionally hostile neighbor Japan and toward the West. Hay succeeds in gaining support from the major powers. Germany, Russia, France, and Japan, for example, all have interests in expanded trade with China. Britain has secretly been advocating its own "open" policy. The problem is that the Chinese themselves are not so enthusiastic. Adams writes a long, sardonic letter to Hay warning that the "Open Door" may be off its hinges and Hay left with nowhere to turn. But Hay persists.

A secret organization of Chinese, called the Righteous and Harmonious Fists (thus referred to as *Boxers* by Westerners) begins to terrorize Christian missionaries whom the Boxers see as representing Western efforts to exploit the nation. In June of 1900, the Dowager Empress officially supports the Boxers and orders that all foreigners be killed. The Legations in Peking (now called Beijing), the Chinese capital, are filled with refugees. Rumors spread that the Boxers have massacred countless refugees, stirring talk of revenge around the world. Through diplomatic channels, Hay manages to spread the word that the Legations are safe. A relief expedition consisting of troops from the major powers occupies Peking on August 14, forcing China to agree to peace terms. Hay insists on the territorial and administrative integrity of China. China is forced to pay damages, but Hay sees to it that the United States uses its share to provide scholarships to Chinese students who want to study in America. He writes Adams that he feels it is worth all the risks to be a part of the opening of China, an issue that will still be controversial more than a century later.

McKinley is assassinated in September 1901, a few months into his second term. His vice president, Theodore Roosevelt, takes the oath of office on September 14. Under the administrations of McKinley and Roosevelt, with the leadership of Hay, the United States becomes a prestigious international power. In 1901, Hay also negotiates the Hay-Pauncefote Treaty, opening the way for the construction of the Panama Canal.

Character Insight

Adams sees that the science and technology of his youth are in their twilight and accepts the dawn of the age of electricity with mixed feelings. He continues his early efforts to formulate a new understanding of history. He sees *unity* in medieval Christianity. God is one: The cross, the chalice, the Gothic cathedral and the Virgin all are one. In the new science, he sees *multiplicity*. Education in the new era tends toward complexity, even confusion, which he sees as necessary and positive. The opposite of confusion is not clarity but ignorance. Henry looks to the German philosopher Hegel (1770–1831) and his theory of historical development. Put simply, Hegel maintains that development begins with a thesis. In opposition to it is an antithesis. This conflict results in a synthesis, which serves as the future thesis, to be confronted in the next step. According to the Hegelian approach, the old thesis here is unity. The new antithesis is multiplicity. Henry cannot see what the future synthesis will be; to him, in 1901, it appears to be chaos: "He admitted that, for the moment, the darkness was dense. He could not affirm with confidence, even to himself, that his 'largest synthesis' would certainly turn out to be chaos, since he would be equally obliged to deny the chaos." If Adams seems confusing as the reader struggles to understand, keep in mind that he, too, is struggling and confused. He begins by saying that the answer he seeks probably does not exist. The approach is filled with paradox: Learning results in ignorance; ignorance is wisdom; order leads to chaos. Adams would not be disappointed if his readers came away with the conclusion that the only truth is that there is no truth. At this point, perhaps it all amounts to *Teufelsdröckh*. But Adams has not finished his search for a theory of history. Indeed, he has barely begun.

Glossary

Teufelsdröckh (German) devil's dung. The central character in Thomas Carlyle's *Sartor Resartus* (1836).

paroxysm a sudden attack, as of a disease or a sudden outburst, as of laughter.

opprobrium the disgrace or infamy attached to shameful conduct.

culbute (French) somersault; downfall.

ontologist one who studies ontology, the branch of metaphysics dealing with the nature of being or reality.

orthodox conforming to the usual beliefs or established doctrines.

Götterdämmerung (German) twilight of the Gods; the total, usually violent, collapse of a society, regime, or institution.

philistine a person regarded as smugly narrow and conventional in views and taste.

Chapter XXVIII
(The Height of Knowledge)

Summary

Adams briefly comments on the "hideous political murders" of three Presidents of the United States assassinated in office in Henry's lifetime: Abraham Lincoln (1865), James Garfield (1881), and William McKinley (1901). He sees 1901 as a year of tragedy, including the deaths of John Hay's son, Del, and one of Henry's best friends, Clarence King. Adams occasionally demonstrates remarkable prescience regarding political developments in the coming century, here accurately predicting the importance of Germany's relationship with France and England. Henry's theory of history continues to develop within the context of paradox.

Commentary

As the new century progresses, Adams becomes nearly obsessed with endings and beginnings, deaths and rebirths. At the age of sixty-four, he sees his own life, and the life of his generation, in its twilight. He and his young country have lived through three presidential assassinations; the lesson, if any, is that life goes on. "America has always taken tragedy lightly," he observes; the country is too busy with progress to mourn long. He mentions a nation of "twenty-million-horse-power," indicating the beginning of a new age; the horsepower of the motors in a single city will surpass this number within a few decades. Clarence King's demise especially saddens him because King was "the best and brightest" of Henry's generation. All of this is significant because Adams is reevaluating his life as well as his view of history. Part of Henry's response is admittedly personal, but it comes at a time when the world is changing even more dramatically than usual.

Adams often is at his best when he discusses politics or higher education. In this chapter, he demonstrates remarkable foresight regarding Europe in the twentieth century: "Either Germany must destroy England and France to create the next inevitable unification as a system of continent against continent—or she must pool interests." It would take two world wars and nearly ninety years for the nations involved to figure that out—the "unification" finally attempted through the European Union. England's Winston Churchill will see things Adams's way before 1950, but even that influential figure cannot gather enough support to bring Europe together.

The chapter's title can be understood only as part of a paradox: The height of knowledge is the abyss of ignorance. By that, Adams means that a person really cannot know anything until he realizes that he knows nothing. He finds this to be especially true as a historian in 1902. Values are reversed, as the old knowledge is found inadequate. Out of the abyss will come Henry's new, dynamic theory of history. Within this context, Adams begins to divide the social evolution of mankind into what Ernest Samuels calls a "complex power system resembling a kind of gravitational field." According to Henry's theory, the first phase of development ran from the beginning of time until 3,000 B.C., about the date of the pyramids. This involved the biological evolution of the species and the gathering of forces such as fire, language, religion, domesticated animals, and milled grain used for food. The second phase in what Adams calls his "chart of relations" ran to about 1,000 A.D. and was involved primarily with learning to use force and energy more economically. Adams later will mention development of metals, more sophisticated use of tools, and the spread of writing as examples of this period. The third phase ran to about 1800. Here the Church reigned as force but began declining under secular influences and emphasis on a nature-centered rather than God-centered universe; the importance of science exacerbated the Church's situation. Mechanical forces began to take over during the fourth phase, running from 1800 to 1900. Henry is not able to see the future clearly. He is still working toward his dynamic theory, the beginning of which must be recognition of the abyss of ignorance.

Glossary

Ça vous amuse, la vie?   (French) So, does life amuse you? (Here, stated ironically.)

neurosis   any of various mental disorders including anxiety, compulsions, phobias, and depression.

Lucius Seneca   (4 BC–AD 65) Roman philosopher, dramatist, and statesman. Ordered to commit suicide by his former student and supposed friend, Nero Claudius.

Nero Claudius   (AD 37–68) emperor of Rome (54–68), notoriously cruel and depraved.

wanton   undisciplined; unmanageable.

Chapter XXIX
(The Abyss of Ignorance)

Summary

Henry continues to struggle toward a scientific understanding of history. He now sees lines of force in the actions of mankind where he once saw lines of will. Henry reconsiders the concepts of unity and multiplicity and wonders if these apparent opposites may not be the same thing. He studies this possibility within the concept of the kinetic theory of gases with startling results. Placing a great deal of importance on unity and multiplicity, he begins to write his *Mont-Saint-Michel and Chartres* (privately printed 1904); he will ultimately think of *The Education of Henry Adams* (first private edition published in 1907) as its companion piece.

Commentary

Theme

After he has realized that the height of the old knowledge is really the abyss of ignorance, Henry has found a starting point for the development of his dynamic theory of history. He feels certain that there is a relationship between the lines of force studied in new science and the lines of force in history. Perhaps disingenuously, the narrator claims that Henry begins to see "lines of force all about him, where he had always seen lines of will," *independently* but in the manner of Michael Faraday, the English physicist who discovered electromagnetic induction in 1831. Faraday proved that electrical charges are subject to polarity, leading to the invention of the dynamo. Adams has mentioned Faraday's work in Chapter XXVI ("Twilight") and has employed the dynamo as a symbol of modern multiplicity in Chapter XXV ("The Virgin and the Dynamo"), but here, the narrator dubiously claims that Henry has never heard of Faraday and comes to his observations independently.

The significance of force versus will is that the former allows for a dynamic, mechanical, scientific motive to the direction of history instead of relying on maxims like "God's will be done" or "it's God's will," which were adequate for the medieval churchman. Adams suggests that Thomas Aquinas, for example, may say, "To me, Christ and the Mother are one Force—Love—simple, single, and sufficient for all human wants." The force for Aquinas is God's will manifested through love. But as science progresses, the force is understood in more complex ways. There are many forces, and one understands them through scientific theories or formulae. One is the kinetic theory of gases, which Henry finds instructive. Molecules of gas exist in each portion of space. What looks like a unit is really a vast complex of molecules and movement. Henry is impressed that the molecules fly at each other at speeds up to a mile a second, colliding as many as 17,750,000 times a second. This is a world in flux. Scientific "unity" thus is made up of millions of molecules, all in motion. As Henry concludes, "[T]he scientific synthesis commonly called unity [is] the scientific analysis commonly called multiplicity." For the scientist, then, unity and multiplicity are the same phenomena. Henry wonders how this can apply to the study of history. He is beginning to believe that man is no longer a projection of God's will or even a manifestation of man's will. In one of his more entertaining metaphors, Adams suggests that man is "an acrobat, with a dwarf on his back, crossing a chasm on a slack rope, and commonly breaking his neck." More seriously, Henry is beginning to believe that mankind is part of the flux and subject to rules of force and motion.

From the abyss of ignorance, Henry seeks understanding consistent with the new science. He sees two helpful points of reference. One is the medieval century from 1150 to 1250 from which he "might measure motion down to his own time, without assuming anything as true or untrue, except relation." He sets himself the task of writing the *Mont-Saint-Michel and Chartres*, which he here subtitles, "a study of thirteenth-century unity." The second point of perspective will be the *Education*, which, we know from his letters, is actually thought of as he is working on the first volume of *Chartres*; it is not yet part of the plan. He subtitles this second work, "a study of twentieth-century multiplicity."

Glossary

coquetry   flirting.

vis a tergo   (Latin) force from behind.

kinetic   of or caused by motion.

metaphysics   the branch of philosophy that seeks to explain the nature of being or reality (ontology) and the origin and structure of the universe (cosmology); it is closely related to the study of the nature of knowledge (epistemology).

Chapter XXX (Vis Inertiae)

Summary

Adams turns his attention back to international politics and his friend John Hay, now at "the summit of his career." Henry attempts to speak of the political influence of nations in terms of inertia and is specifically interested in Russia, China, and the Russo-Japanese War. He fears that the Open Door to China is about to be closed, perhaps permanently. Adams discusses his attitude toward women and comments on the emancipation of the gender in America in the early 1900s as well as the dangers that he thinks this entails. He mentions women's "superiority" but in a somewhat patronizing and limited way.

Commentary

Adams is an expert on international politics; his observations regarding the current scene, as well as the coming century, are always worth noting. John Hay has been brilliant in his efforts to open China to international commerce and to maintain its integrity after the Boxer Rebellion. However, Henry worries that this success may be threatened by the ambitions of two emerging modern powers: Russia and Japan. Japan sees itself as the dominant nation in Asia; it has already established economic influence in Korea and hopes to gain a strong foothold on the Chinese mainland. Russia is also interested in establishing control in China. Having invested military interests in Manchuria during the Boxer Rebellion, Russia (since 1898) has leased the seaport of Port Arthur (now Lüshun) in Liaoning province, the intent being to establish a center for Russian naval power in the Pacific. Tensions increase in 1903 as Russia refuses to withdraw its troops from Manchuria or to recognize Japan's interests. The Japanese attack Port Arthur on February 8, 1904 and blockade the Russian fleet. With superior naval power and effective use of land forces, Japan has the better of the war. The United States brokers a peace treaty on September 5, 1905, stipulating that Russia must withdraw from Manchuria and surrender its base at Port Arthur.

Henry's initial concern is that China will be closed to international trade. Six days after the Japanese surprise attack on Port Arthur, he writes Elizabeth Cameron that "the 8th of February will be a pretty serious and solemn anniversary I reckon, a good while after I have done my yawp." Henry further fears that Germany will be drawn into Asian interests by the inertia and gravitational pull of Russia. He hopes that Germany can be held in the Atlantic system, sharing interests with England and France, as Hay has arranged after several years of maneuvering. If Germany's interests are drawn away, Adams correctly anticipates "a century of friction" in Europe. He also wisely warns that, in the long run, Russia may be an even greater threat to Western interests than Germany will be.

Character Insight

As prescient and insightful as Adams can be regarding international affairs, his insistence on applying laws of force or mass to the movements of economics or diplomacy is less fruitful. As a metaphor, inertia may be of some interest; but the attempt to approach international politics, let alone world history, as if it were a scientific study of matter is more ambitious than informing. Here, for example, one may expect Russia to defeat Japan easily, considering only mass and inertia, but Japan wins the war. The reader may wish that Adams could just share his considerable political insight and not be quite so impressed with the methods of modern science.

When it comes to women, Adams is a hopeless romantic and idealist. In his letters to Elizabeth, for example, and often throughout the *Education* (including this chapter), he speaks of the "superiority" of women; but he does so with such grand chivalry that one wonders about the practical application of his evaluation. At best, women have a function in the home, the Church, and perhaps the arts for Henry. The ideal woman would seem to be the Madonna. He places women on a pedestal, which may be reverent from Adams's viewpoint but is out of step with the political and economic interests of actual American women in the early twentieth century.

Theme

At this point, women are struggling just to get the vote in the States. (The nineteenth amendment to the United States Constitution, passed August 18, 1920, will finally allow for women's suffrage.) With the industrial revolution, they seek a place in the workforce. Adams acknowledges the latter when he speaks of women who work as typists, clerks, factory hands, and "telegraph-girls." He warns, however, that joining the work force is abandoning "the cradle and the family."

To succeed, he concludes, women "must become sexless like the bees." As much as he avows that women are superior, it would rarely occur to Henry, or most men in his generation, to have women serve in the Senate, in the House of Representatives, or on the board of a major corporation. Henry would say that women are far too fine for the nasty old worlds of politics or commerce. In practical terms, it is false flattery, more restricting than liberating. Henry's attitude toward women may better be evaluated by their scarce representation in the *Education*. He does say that he has learned more from women than from men, which begs the questions, "Which women educated him and in what way?" The reader never knows. Aside from that and a few mentions of women in domestic or social roles, there is little about women in the *Education*.

Glossary

vis inertiae   (Latin) the force of inertia, later simply referred to as "inertia," the tendency of matter to remain at rest if at rest or to stay in motion if in motion.

enigma   a perplexing, usually ambiguous, statement; a riddle.

Mikado   the emperor of Japan, a title no longer used.

Cassini   Count Arthur P. Cassini, Russian ambassador to the United States in 1903.

vis nova   (Latin) new force.

ostentatiously   in a showy manner.

Chapter XXXI
(The Grammar of Science)

Summary

Karl Pearson's classic approach to scientific method, *The Grammar of Science*, first published in 1899, evokes both praise and condemnation from Adams. Henry deletes some of his stronger criticism from the 1907 edition of *Education*; but his written opinions, criticizing scientists for their reluctance to draw broad conclusions, exist elsewhere, including the margins of his copy of Pearson's book. Pearson emphasizes the importance of experiments, measurements, and observation. He is remembered as the first scientist to use statistics extensively in biological science, a practice soon extended to the social sciences. Adams observes that the only conclusion science offers is "ultimate chaos. In plain words, Chaos was the law of nature; Order was the dream of man." Henry seeks something more.

Commentary

As Ernest Samuels points out, "By this time in the *Education,* 'historian' obviously had become to Adams a generic name for speculative philosopher or metaphysician." Prior to this, Henry has looked to the past for unity, speaking nostalgically of the guidance of the Virgin and the Church in medieval philosophy. Although he is impressed with scientific method and would like to apply it to the study of history, Adams is annoyed with scientists such as Pearson because they see their roles as observers, measurers, and recorders. They refuse to make judgments about ultimate reality beyond what they can observe and measure. The passage that Adams expurgates from his *Education* condemns Pearson for being overly devoted to experimentation and measurement; Henry wants some ultimate answers, a guide to metaphysics. In one of his better-known epigrams, Adams writes, "No one means all he says, and yet very few say all they mean." He wants scientists to say more, to become philosophers along with the ideal historian.

Theme

Formerly, Adams points out, mankind could count on such certainties as "Unity, Continuity, Purpose, Order, Law, Truth, the Universe, God"; science takes these away and replaces them with "Multiplicity, Diversity, Complexity, Anarchy, Chaos." Adams admires the method, but the conclusion—or lack of one—at least privately annoys him. On the other hand, he offers this caveat: "The historian must not try to know what is truth, if he values his honesty; for, if he cares for his truths, he is certain to falsify his facts." To this extent, then, he accepts scientific method, in that he realizes that the result must come from observation and not *a priori*. But he does seek some conclusion, some guide through the maze of chaos. He is close to the creation of his "Dynamic Theory of History."

Glossary

Civitas Dei, Civitas Romae (Latin) City of God, City of Rome; the former refers to Saint Augustine's (354–430) *De civitate Dei*; the latter is a secular reference.

simian of or like an ape or monkey.

fecund fruitful or fertile.

aperture an opening, hole, or gap.

fabulist a person who writes or tells fables.

Chapter XXXII (Vis Nova)

Summary and Commentary

Adams has spent most of the last third of his book dealing with new science; to the reader's benefit, he is also concerned with international politics. Here, the author uses the term *vis nova* (new force) to describe not only scientific advance but also the new role of the United States in the international scene. Returning from Paris, Henry is in for a shock: "On January 6, 1904, he reached Washington, where the contrast of atmosphere astonished him, for he had never before seen his country think as a world power." As if to remind the reader of the importance of history, Henry returns to the topic of Chapter XXX, the Russo-Japanese War, and Secretary of State Hay's interest in keeping China's doors open. As Jean Gooder points out, Adams is friendly with Russia's Count Cassini; but his sympathies lie with the Japanese. If Russia's "inertia" moves it into a controlling position in Southeast Asia, Henry fears, China may be closed to the West for a long time. Japan is no innocent bystander; its military rivalry with China and Korea is traditional and will last at least another forty years. But Adams agrees with Hay that it is in the West's best interest to keep Russia out. The Anglo-Japanese alliance of 1902 puts Japan in a better position to confront Russia because of the support of England. Adams welcomes the success of the Open Door policy; he agrees with Hay that the West needs improved trade with China. The policy, says Adams, is Hay's "last great triumph." Henry's dear friend and neighbor will die on July 1, 1905.

Character Insight

Henry witnesses the scientific aspect of *vis nova* at the St. Louis World's Fair of 1904, timed to celebrate the centennial of the Louisiana Purchase (actually 1803). Ever the New Englander, Adams finds the Midwest reeking with smoke and crawling with dirty suburbs: "Evidently, cleanliness was not to be the birthmark of the new American." St. Louis, he concludes, is "a third-rate town of half-a-million people without history, education, unity or art." But he is impressed by the overwhelming pageantry produced by electricity: "The world had never witnessed so marvelous a phantasm . . . a glow half so astonishing . . . long lines of white palaces, exquisitely lighted by thousands on thousands of electric candles, soft, rich, shadowy, palpable." This is the third

86

exposition (Chicago, Paris) that has overwhelmed Henry with the burgeoning force of science. To understand his awe, one needs only to live briefly in a world without electricity. As he approaches his seventieth year, Adams feels pressed for time. He feels he must "account to himself for himself somehow" and "invent a formula of his own for his universe." Adams claims he is not looking for absolute truth but merely "a spool on which to wind the thread of history without breaking it." The spool will be his "Dynamic Theory of History."

Glossary

disconcerted   frustrated, confused, or embarrassed.

iniquity   wickedness; lack of righteousness or justice.

Fête Dieu   (French) God's Festival; the Feast of Corpus Christi, a festival celebrated on the Thursday or Sunday after Trinity Sunday, in honor of the Eucharist.

seneschal   a steward or major-domo (chief steward) in the household of a medieval noble.

Chapter XXXIII (A Dynamic Theory of History) and Chapter XXXIV (A Law of Acceleration)

Summary

Adams approaches the entire span of mankind's history on earth from the point of view of "progress" and "forces," for which he has specific definitions. His theory "defines Progress as the development and economy of forces." "Force" can be anything that produces work; but he also speaks, perhaps more importantly, of the "attractive force" of opposing bodies, the gravitational pull of an entity. He applies his theory to what he considers to be the major divisions of history. The first runs from the dawn of time to 3000 B.C. (the date of the pyramids). Second is the period from 3000 B.C. to 1000 A.D., concerned primarily with economies of energy rather than their development, according to Adams. The era from 1000 to 1800 features declining energy of the Church and increasing interest in science. In the nineteenth century, scientific discovery begins to grow. Finally, Adams is concerned about the future, which will require a new kind of intelligence.

Commentary

The central metaphor of Adams's dynamic theory is the gravitational attraction of an entity. This is a *dynamic* theory because it considers concepts, as well as objects, to be constantly in motion; in flux, not static. Adams is interested in social and intellectual movement, the *evolution* of mankind from the dawn of time to 1900 and, speculatively, beyond. He covers this in about fourteen pages. Students should not be surprised if he seems abstract or, at times, confusing. The top Adams scholar of the twentieth century, Ernest Samuels, in *The Major Phase*, even wonders if the entire, extreme approach may be satire; he is sympathetic with students who may wonder what is going on and asks, "Who is not lost in wild surmise at the crux?"

However, you need not remain lost. To find your way through the maze, hold onto that central metaphor: the gravitational attraction of an entity. Adams is saying that, from the beginning, mankind has been drawn to the "attractive force" of various concepts. Man is not shaping nature; nature is interacting with mankind. The earliest man was different from Darwin's apes or monkeys, according to Adams, because he was able to respond to higher "forces" or concepts; they attracted his capacity to learn. There have been various stages of attraction: survival, power, philosophy, and the appeal of divinity were among the most important through the year 1000. Mankind was drawn to these as if by a gravitational pull, distinguishing him from other primates: "Susceptibility to the highest forces is the highest genius; selection between them is the highest science; their mass is the highest educator."

From 1000 to 1800, Adams sees mankind as drawn more toward scientific experimentation in the natural world; the attraction of theology waned. This attraction to scientific investigation increased in the nineteenth century at such an exponential rate that Adams is concerned about mankind's capacity to keep up during the next (twentieth) century.

Adams feels that the laws of acceleration may provide scientific force that is too much for the human mind. If the attraction of scientific information continues to increase at the current rate, mankind will have to make some sort of intellectual leap to keep up. Sometimes Adams's examples seem absurd. For example, he bases his rate of scientific expansion on the increased use of coal power between 1800 and 1900, a convenient doubling every ten years or so. On the other hand, his predictions are often amazingly accurate. He anticipates that the scientific body of information is increasing so quickly that the human brain will be unable to keep up. With a *leap of intellect*, however, he thinks that Americans in the year 2000 would be able to "control unlimited power" and "think in complexities unimaginable to an earlier mind." One could now say that the leap of intellect that Adams anticipates is, in fact, accomplished through use of the computer and artificial intelligence. Adams is right. He is also prescient about the dangers as well as positive potential of nuclear power, stating that power comes from every atom, "enough of it to supply the stellar universe. . . . Man could no longer hold it off."

Throughout these chapters, Adams relies on two guides that are important to his process and, therefore, his conclusions. The English philosopher, essayist and statesman Francis Bacon (1561–1626) directs him with his belief that truth is discovered through empirical observation, which is compatible with the approach of Pearson (Chapter XXXI) and his contemporaries. Speaking of Bacon, Adams writes, "He urged society to lay aside the idea of evolving the universe from a thought, and to try evolving thought from the universe."

When considering mankind's future, Adams compares the orbit of the Great Comet of 1843 to the path of humankind as it approaches the twentieth century. Although he is incorrect in thinking that the spectacular comet moved "in defiance of [natural] law," Adams helpfully infers from the comet a need for man's leap of intellect to project the human mind into a sphere of understanding congruent with the amount of new knowledge. As the comet is attracted to the sun, which Adams thinks it orbits with a leap, the mind of man is attracted to scientific inquiry. The central metaphor of gravitational attraction holds throughout.

Glossary

fetish   here, any object believed by superstitious people to have magical power.

audaciously   boldly, fearlessly.

In hoc signo vinces!   (Latin) In (or through) this sign, you will conquer! (Said of the Cross.)

ignominy   loss of one's reputation; shame and dishonor; infamy.

ordnance   cannon or artillery.

dynamometer   an apparatus for measuring force or power.

antinomy   a contradiction or inconsistency between two laws, principles, and so on.

Chapter XXXV (Nunc Age)

Summary and Commentary

In this short, concluding chapter, Adams briefly mentions scientific power and politics, but despite the forward-looking chapter title, *Nunc Age* (Latin for "Now, take action!"), his focus really is on the past and on endings. On November 5, 1904, as he approaches New York City, returning from yet another trip to Europe, Henry is excited by the vitality of the great city, which "became frantic in its effort to explain something that defied meaning. Power seemed to have outgrown its servitude and to have asserted its freedom." This is the age that he has anticipated in the last third of the *Education*, but he leaves the work of the future to the next generation. Adams feels that he and his contemporaries are near the end. Clarence King died—broken—in 1901; John Hay is in poor shape and, despite Henry's efforts, dies on July 1, 1905. Three days later, Henry writes to Mrs. Hay to express condolences and reflect on the twilight of his own life: "I had not the heart to telegraph. All the world will have done that, and will have overwhelmed you with messages of condolence. I can say nothing. You will understand it. . . . As for me, it is time to bid good-bye. I am tired. My last hold on the world is lost with him." Adams has privately printed the *Mont-Saint-Michel and Chartres* in 1904; the first private edition of the *Education* will come out in 1907. He will write a little more in the next few years, but he suffers a disabling stroke in 1912 and dies on March 27, 1918.

However, the story of the education of the boy from Boston stops in 1905. Henry wonders, at the end, whether he and his old friends may be allowed to return just for one day—in 1938, say, their centenary—to see the "mistakes of their own lives made clear in the light of the mistakes of their successors." He wistfully wonders if it will be, for the first time in history, a world that "sensitive and timid natures could regard without a shudder." For once, Henry's speculation seems wrong. With Hitler leading the Third Reich into World War II, and Hiroshima and Nagasaki soon to come, 1938 will be no time for timid natures. But having completed this journey with him, the reader knows that Henry already suspects something like that.

Glossary

querulous   inclined to find fault; complaining.

repine   to feel or express unhappiness or discontent.

"The rest is silence."   Hamlet's dying words (V, ii, 372) in William Shakespeare's tragedy *Hamlet, Prince of Denmark* (1600–1601).

assent   agree; concur.

CHARACTER ANALYSES

Henry Adams

The narrator is quick to point out that few people born in 1838 find themselves in more favorable circumstances than Henry Adams. The grandson of one President of the United States and great-grandson of another, Henry inherits a respected family name, automatic contacts with some of the most powerful people in the country, and financial security. As impressive as all that is, however, it is not the reason that we know about him today. What sets Henry apart is his intellectual curiosity. In discussing his "Dynamic Theory of History" (Chapter XXXIII), Adams suggests that mankind began to evolve beyond the apes because of a capacity to respond to the "attractive forces" that one may over-simply call knowledge. "Susceptibility to the highest forces is the highest genius; selection between them is the highest science; their mass is the highest educator," Adams says. Because of his unusual intellectual curiosity, Henry is more attracted than most to "highest forces," the ultimate levels of knowledge. That is his genius. He is interested in almost everything around him, and this interest helps him to distinguish, to select, between mundane and worthwhile pursuits. This is the one constant throughout his life.

As a young boy, Henry is attracted to the same things that attract most children. He prefers diversity, freedom, the "endless delight" of sensual impressions, and occasional "outlawry." But by the time he travels to Washington with his father in 1850, he is already becoming curious about larger issues. His first impressions of slavery shock him: "Slavery struck him in the face; it was a nightmare; a horror; a crime; the sum of all wickedness!" He wants to escape, along with the slaves, to free soil. His curiosity takes him beyond immediate impressions, some of which are actually pleasant. It occurs to him that the casual, relaxed life of the indolent South is paid for by human bondage. Especially upsetting and confusing is the trip to George Washington's home, Mount Vernon. Henry realizes that the father of his country, the man he has thought of as beyond reproach, was supported by slavery. At the age of twelve, Henry can't understand what exactly this adds up to; does it mean that Washington was an evil man? Henry ultimately slides into the uncomfortable, insufficient conclusion that Washington was unique. For the confused child, Washington just wasn't like other men; he "stood alone." Henry's education has not prepared him for further understanding.

Throughout his life, Henry protests against the limitations of formal education. His undergraduate years at Harvard (1854–1858) and his brief attempt at a legal education in Berlin (1858–1859) convince him that there is too much emphasis on rote memory and too little cultivation of legitimate intellectual curiosity in most educational systems. Henry is only an average student at Harvard, but he does begin to excel at expressing himself. He contributes to *Harvard Magazine* and is chosen Class Orator as a senior. In Berlin, his interest in learning the language causes him to attend a German prep school for a term, studying with boys several years his junior. While he finds German education even more repressive than that in the States, Henry does become fluent in the language and is seen reading novels and other books in German on his own during his "Grand Tour" of Europe.

As an assistant professor of history at Harvard (1870–1877), Henry takes advantage of an opportunity to improve higher education. Although he claims that his effort is a "failure," Adams introduces several innovative approaches that stand the test of time. His own intellectual curiosity causes him to experiment with liberating the curiosity of his students. Adams feels that the lecture system, which he never liked as a student, is not working for him as a teacher. Part of the reason is that he is not sufficiently expert in the medieval history classes that he is teaching; but the main problem is that one-way communication, lecturing professor dictating to note-taking students, is stultifying. In an honors class with only half a dozen students, Henry tries something different. He experiments with a seminar system, allowing the students to read on their own and bring what they have learned to the class, engaging their own intellectual curiosity. It works. The students are more involved and cover more material in a strikingly vital way. They inform and confront each other. Henry only wishes he had a second professor in the class to debate with him. The classes meet at Henry's private rooms rather than the lecture hall. He also introduces graduate studies in history at Harvard, encourages the study of American history, and encourages student evaluations as well as the keeping of journals. He complains that the regular system fails because no teacher can effectively work with more than six students at a time; most classes are much larger because of financial restraints, limiting the possibilities for real learning.

As a political journalist, Henry is drawn to reform. Serving as a freelance writer in Washington (1868–1870), he is especially interested in financial matters, seeking to overturn the creation of the "greenback" dollar and investigating the New York gold conspiracy. During the Civil War, the federal government issued greenback dollars, paper currency that was not supported by gold. Henry journalistically argues that this was unconstitutional and advocates their removal; the Supreme Court ultimately rules in favor of the greenback. The Gold Scandal of 1869 especially piques Henry's curiosity as he suspects collusion between Jay Gould and members of the Grant administration. Gould tries to corner the market on gold bullion and coin but falls just short as Secretary of Treasury Boutwell finally places on sale $4,000,000 worth of government gold. Suspiciously, Gould seems to have known about the government intervention beforehand and sells his gold at a substantial profit just in time. Although the involvement of the Grant administration is never proven, Henry uncovers Gould's part in the gold conspiracy while Henry's brother Charles investigates corruption in the management of the railroads.

The panic of 1893 draws Henry into another controversy, this over the gold standard. Eager to expand the economy and cheapen currency, Henry argues that international trade contracts and the American economy should be based on a combination of gold and silver, not on gold alone. Although born an American aristocrat, he finds himself supporting the position of farmers and small businessmen because he fears a new ruling class of bankers and gold capitalists (whom he calls *goldbugs*). Henry is drawn to what he sees as a higher wisdom, a "susceptibility to the highest forces [being] the highest genius." With similar justification, he advocates independence for Cuba, which is liberated from Spain in the Spanish-American War of 1898.

Henry's curiosity is especially drawn to modern advances in science. Karl Pearson's classic work on scientific method, the *Grammar of Science* (1899) confirms, for Henry, the need to seek knowledge through experimentation and observation rather than working from a premise that the intellect simply tries to prove. Henry is impressed with advances in electricity and mechanical engines. He begins to wonder if the methods of science could be applied successfully to a study of history. At the same time, he has become a devoted student of medieval philosophy and architecture, especially their manifestations in the twelfth and thirteenth centuries. While he is nostalgic for the unity that he sees in medieval Christianity, he realistically anticipates a need to adapt to the multiplicity of modern science. He is drawn to his creation of a "Dynamic Theory of History," which looks at the evolution of mankind as a series of gravitational attractions to "forces" such as knowledge concerning survival, spirituality, and science. In an examination of medieval unity, he writes *Mont-Saint-Michel and Chartres* (1904), a historical, philosophical consideration of thirteenth-century Christianity as symbolized by the architecture and icons of two famous French cathedrals built during the period. As a companion piece, he creates *The Education of Henry Adams* (1907), a study of modern multiplicity as well as the biography of an education.

Henry Adams's rich and productive life is a product of his intellectual curiosity more than any other single factor. While it is true that he was born privileged, so are many others. Readers still find Henry Adams of interest in the twenty-first century because of his achievements, not his birth.

John Hay

It is not surprising that John Hay becomes one of Henry Adams's closest friends. They share political and personal interests as well as similar life experiences; their lives complement each other so well that they build homes next door to each other.

Born in Salem, Indiana, October 8, 1838, and educated at Brown University, Hay gets to know Adams well while serving as assistant secretary of state in 1879–1880. Hay devotes the next seventeen years to writing and shares, with Adams, a passion for history. During the American Civil War (1861–1865), Hay was assistant to John Nicolay, Abraham Lincoln's private secretary. Hay had practiced law next door to Lincoln in Springfield, Illinois, and accompanied the president-elect to Washington. From material collected during this period, Hay and Nicolay write *Abraham Lincoln: a History* in ten volumes (1890). They also publish *Abraham Lincoln: Collected Works* (1894) in two volumes. Hay has also published his own *Pike County Ballads* (1871), a popular collection of poems in frontier dialect. In the mid-1880s, Hay and Adams, and their spouses, build houses next to each other on Lafayette Square in Washington.

Hay returns to public service near the turn of the century and distinguishes himself in the realm of international politics. After serving a year or so as ambassador to Great Britain, Hay is secretary of state for McKinley and Theodore Roosevelt until his death (1898–1905). This is a period of dramatically increasing influence by the United States in international affairs. Hay is in charge of peace negotiations after the Spanish-American War and is instrumental in securing Cuba's independence while annexing the Philippines for the United States, which assures the U. S. of some influence in the Pacific. He is responsible for the "Open Door" policy with China (1899), an attempt to provide trade opportunities for the benefit of the West as well as Japan, Russia, and China. During the Boxer Rebellion (1900), Hay assures Western diplomats that the Legations in Peking are safe. As part of the peace terms, he assures the territorial and administrative integrity of China. When China is forced to pay damages, Hay makes sure that the United States uses its share to provide scholarships to Chinese students who want to study in America. Hay also negotiates the Hay-Pauncefote Treaty (1901), opening the way for the construction of the Panama Canal.

Personally, Adams and Hay are the best of friends. Hay, Adams, their wives, and Clarence King socialize frequently; they call this inner circle "The Five of Hearts." When Hay dies, Adams, in Paris, writes Clara Stone Hay, Hay's widow, touchingly if not altogether accurately, "My last hold on the world is lost with him."

Charles Francis Adams

Charles Francis is an especially strong influence on Henry because the son serves as his father's private secretary for several months in Washington, where the elder Adams is a member of the House of Representatives (1860–1861), and remains in the same position when his father becomes Minister to England (1861–1868). What impresses Henry most is his father's strong, honest character, which carries him through crises small and large.

The reader's first significant view of the elder Adams' influence is during the trip to Washington with Henry in 1850. Charles Francis allows Henry to see slavery for what it is, as much as a twelve-year-old outsider can, and to reach his own conclusions. Henry is shocked and upset, wishing that he could flee to free territory along with the slaves. In the same chapter, the reader witnesses Henry's first political disillusionment. The Free Soil Party, to which his father belongs at the time, negotiates a bargain to support a proslavery democrat for the office of governor of Massachusetts in exchange for democratic support of the Free Soil candidate for United States senator. This is Henry's "first lesson in practical politics" and a shocking one. His one consolation is that his father will have no part of it.

That sort of bold integrity serves the father well. His greatest achievement, in the eyes of history as well as his son's, is his effective management of the politically explosive situation in England during Charles

Francis's tenure as Minister. As soon as he arrives in England, shortly after the beginning of the U. S. Civil War (1861–1865), the Minister learns that England is not supporting the Union, as he expected, but has avowed neutrality. The Minister receives this disturbing news with stoic calm. He is especially adroit at keeping England from formally recognizing the Confederacy and cuts off attempts at aid to the South. For example, when the war in the States is very much in doubt, the Confederacy contracts for two ironclad warships to be built by William Laird & Son in Liverpool. Minister Adams learns of it and sends a series of notes to British Foreign Secretary Lord Russell, protesting the situation. On September 1, 1863, Russell writes the Minister that he cannot interfere with the building of the ships in any way. However, during that summer, the Union has established an upper hand in the war, with victories at Gettysburg and Vicksburg. Adams plays his improved position with candor, responding to Russell in the strongest possible terms: "It would be superfluous in me to point out to your Lordship that this is war!" The situation is resolved. Henry is proud of his father; the men who have preceded him in this distinguished family do shape Henry's character.

Clarence King

The member of his generation whom Henry admires most is Clarence King. King is brilliant and unorthodox, ultimately failing because he takes on too many risks. But when Henry meets him, on a geological expedition in Estes Park in 1871, he judges King to be one of the brightest and the best. King is a brilliant geologist. At the age of thirty, within a year of meeting Adams, King publishes *Mountaineering in the Sierra Nevada* (1872), considered a classic in its time. In 1878, he publishes a significant guide to method, *Systematic Geology*. King is also charismatic, clever, energetic, and humorous. He knows art as well as mining and knows women, the reader is told, as well as either. In fact, King lives a double life that includes a common-law marriage to an African-American woman, almost unheard of in his social stratum during these years shortly after the end of slavery. King is an expert on Cuba and correctly anticipates the rebellion that leads to the Spanish-American War (1898). In many ways, the robust, daring King is everything that Henry Adams is not. Henry is baffled when King loses his financial and mental stability during the financial upheaval of 1893 as the value of silver drops by fifty percent. King has taken too many risks in his mining ventures, and he loses his best supporters to death or their own financial strain. He takes refuge in an asylum but recovers sufficiently to visit Cuba with Adams in 1894. However, he seems to be a ruined man and dies in 1901. For Adams, King remains a brilliant star; Henry seems to deny that his friend's excesses have lead to his destruction.

CRITICAL ESSAY

The Education Of Henry Adams as Experimental Literature: Symbol and Theme

From its inception, Adams thought of the *Education* as an experimental work of literature. A part-time novelist, the author here employs several of the devices of fiction. For example, the story is told through a third-person narrator who rarely goes inside the minds of subjects other than Henry. Henry himself is more of a literary device than a person. Adams tells his readers in the "Preface" of February 16, 1907, that Henry should be thought of as a "manikin, on which the toilet [attire] of education is to be draped in order to show the fit or misfit of the clothes." This is not a biography of a person; it is more a biography of an education: "The object of study is the garment, not the figure." Nor does the story have to rely on fact. Like a good novelist, Adams is more interested in truth, whether the details fit or not, as he reveals when describing Henry's trip to Washington in 1850: "The actual journey may have been quite different, but the actual journey has no interest for education." The method and direction of this literary experiment carry his readers on a journey that is much like that of a novel. For illumination that is suggestive rather than definitive, it often relies on two devices that are found in various types of literature: symbol and theme.

Major Symbols

The narrator often speaks cryptically in the *Education*, implying rather than stating his point explicitly. It is anyone's guess how consciously this is done, but his symbols range from cities to machines to religious icons to an ancient fish.

Adams is as interested in places as he is in people, and sometimes he speaks of places as if they represent all the people in them. Employing one of his favorite devices, contrast, he opens the book with a comparison of two places that were important to Henry as a boy and will continue to be significant throughout the work: Boston and Quincy. For Henry, Boston is and will remain many things that he detests. It represents "confinement, school, rule, discipline; straight, gloomy streets . . . restraint, law, unity." State Street, the financial district of Boston, embodies a side of life that Adams struggles against all his life. As an adult, he feels that too much power is invested in bankers and financial manipulators. Worse, the financial leaders of State Street in Henry's youth are mostly pro-slavery, anathema to Henry. Quincy, on the other hand, represents "liberty, diversity, outlawry, the endless delight of mere sense impressions. . . ." Summers are spent in Quincy; and summer, with the one amusing exception of an appointment with summer school, means freedom to Henry. Just as important, Quincy is the ancestral home of the family. There is no pro-slavery sentiment at Quincy. At the end of the first chapter, the narrator wonders if perhaps Henry should have opted for the "fatted calf" of State Street rather than the journey he is about to take. But there is no doubt that Henry would always choose Quincy, reform, integrity, and freedom.

Other places work symbolically in this experimental book. Washington, D. C., provides its own dichotomy for Henry. On the one hand, it represents hope and democracy. On the other, Washington too often stands for practical politics, frustration, and even corruption. An example of each is the first Grant administration (1869–1873), beginning, as Henry thinks it does, with bright possibility but soon turning to lethargy, compromise and the apparent malfeasance linking it to Jay Gould's attempt to corner the gold market in September 1869. Still, Henry does ultimately choose to settle in Washington. It is, after all, the center of political action for the country and, increasingly, the world; and Henry, for all his denial, thrives on politics.

The cities of Europe represent a mixture of values. When Henry first visits Berlin (1858), ostensibly to study law, it has not yet experienced the renaissance that will make it an outstanding world city. At this time, it is notoriously unsanitary. To Henry, it represents the side of the German character that is dull, repressive, and dogmatic. Paris and Rome, in contrast, are inspiring in aesthetic and spiritual ways. Henry will become accustomed to spending summers in Paris even in his later years when his health is in question. But it is London that Henry talks about most in the *Education*. Indulging in a favorite ploy of paradox, the narrator presents some of his infamous English stereotypes at the beginning of Chapter XII: "The English mind was one-sided, eccentric, systematically unsystematic and logically illogical. The less one knew of it the better." Henry carries a family resentment of the English that is left over from the American Revolution and exacerbated by social and political conditions in London during the American Civil War. However, his heritage and his concept of legal justice are British. London represents a mixed bag of values for Henry. Devoted as he is to complexity, it is the perfect place for him to grow to maturity.

Cuba is the only third-world locale visited in the *Education*, but it is not Henry's only island experience. During the twenty years that the narrator skips (1872–1892), Adams traveled extensively in the South Seas with John La Farge, visiting, among other places, Hawaii, Samoa, Tahiti, and Fiji. Henry had a typical Westerner's fascination with island life and even wrote a pseudo-autobiographical work based on his experience, *Memoirs of Marau Taaroa, Last Queen of Tahiti* (1893). To Henry, the islands represent extreme freedom, life without the restrictions of his home civilization; if he sometimes seems patronizing, that is part of the stereotype of the time as well as a reflection of his personality.

Two of the most important symbols in the *Education* have to do with time and philosophy rather than place: the Virgin and the dynamo. For Henry, the Virgin represents the comforting unity that the Church offered in the Middle Ages. In his studies of medieval philosophy and architecture, Henry finds a stable point of view in which the purpose of man is clearly identified; God and the Church and mankind all form a single entity, providing clarity of direction and moral purpose. While he is not personally devoted to any single religion, Adams views medieval life with nostalgia. The icons of the Church—the gothic cathedral, communion, and the cross—provide tactile representation of God's love for man and mankind's responsibility to a higher meaning. The dynamo, a generator for producing electric current, represents modern science and the multiplicity of contemporary philosophy to Adams. While he may not prefer it, Henry believes that science is replacing religion as the dominating force in the lives of mankind. In his "Dynamic Theory of History," Adams argues that religion, the magnetic force that attracted mankind in the Middle Ages, has been replaced steadily, throughout the nineteenth century, by the force of science. He sees the future as an enormous chaos of scientific force that mankind will not deter but can only manage by making some sort of leap of intellect. This is the dilemma that occupies Henry during the last several chapters of the *Education*.

Perhaps the most charming symbol in the *Education* is the *Pteraspis,* "cousin of the sturgeon," a fossil of a jawless fish that existed some 400 million years ago. During a discussion of evolution, the noted geologist Sir Charles Lyell tells Henry that the first vertebrate was "a very respectable fish, among the earliest of all fossils, which had lived, and whose bones were still reposing, under Adams's own favorite Abbey on Wenlock Edge." Henry is delighted. Throughout the work, he refers to *Pteraspis* as to an old friend who represents permanence and continuity, a heritage beyond the limitations of Boston, London, or Berlin. "To an American in search of a father," the narrator tells us, "it mattered nothing whether the father breathed through lungs, or walked on fins, or on feet." Adams loves the esoteric, and the *Pteraspis* is made for him. If it had not existed, he would have had to invent it. It is a literary symbol, the sort of device one might find in a novel rather than a history or a biography and, therefore, appropriate to this experimental hybrid that the author is creating.

Major Themes

Adams also employs themes in the manner of a novelist or even a musical composer. He introduces the theme and then returns to it, embellishing and augmenting as he goes. Important examples in the *Education* are loss of innocence, confronting exploitation, the Christian unity of the Middle Ages, and the scientific multiplicity of the modern era, each of which contributes to Henry's education.

Adams's understanding of "education" has more to do with experience than formal schooling. A step in gaining that experience is the loss of innocence that Henry encounters early in the work. In the opening chapters, readers find a young boy like many others, naïvely enjoying the freedoms of life and rather crossly annoyed by the restrictions. Henry's early life in Quincy, and for the most part in Boston, is innocent and carefree. His view of the world begins to change during his trip to Washington—and the slave states of Maryland and Virginia—with his father in 1850 (Chapter III). This sudden exposure to evil confuses Henry: "The more he was educated, the less he understood." Man's inhumanity to man is appalling, even to this twelve-year-old boy. He wants to flee the nightmare horror of slavery, the "sum of all wickedness." A political deal struck by some leaders of the Free Soil Party further disillusions Henry. They agree to support a pro-slavery democrat for the office of Governor of Massachusetts in exchange for democratic support of the Free Soil candidate for United States Senate. The narrator points out that this is Henry's "first lesson in practical politics." It is not his last. Any remnants of political innocence are stripped away during Henry's years in London (1861–1868).

As the Civil War worsens for the Union, the diplomatic situation in London is exacerbated (Chapter X). The narrator raises the question whether any politician can be trusted. Examples are Prime Minister Palmerston and the British Foreign Secretary, Lord Russell. With the South apparently on the brink of chasing President Lincoln from the White House, Palmerston writes Russell (September 14) and suggests diplomatic intervention on the side of the Confederacy. Russell responds even more strongly; he adamantly supports intervention regardless of the military situation. As the Union gains military advantage, Palmerston backs down. Russell, however, calls for a Cabinet meeting in hopes of intervention. He deceivingly tells Minister Adams that the policy of the British government simply is to "adhere to a strict neutrality." The cabinet votes down Russell's plan for intervention. All along, Henry has trusted Russell, whom the Minister, Charles Francis Adams, has liked but wisely not completely trusted. Russell has behaved like a practical politician, a lesson in experience for Henry.

Having lost his childhood innocence, Henry is prepared for his part in the struggle to confront exploitation of the weak and disenfranchised. This comes as second nature to him because of his experience with slavery and the family's position on that issue during the Civil War. He gets an opportunity to act during his early days as a reform journalist. On September 24, 1869, the price of gold crashes spectacularly, exposing a scheme involving financiers Jay Gould and James Fisk as well as President Grant's brother-in-law, a man named Corbin. Gould and Fisk attempt to corner the market on gold, which would ruin many small investors. The Secretary of the Treasury finally places $4,000,000 worth of government gold on sale, putting an end to the scheme. Gould, however, has somehow learned of the move beforehand and begins to sell just in time. The implication is that Gould had information from inside the Grant cabinet. Although he can never absolutely prove that connection, Henry's investigation into the scheme establishes his reputation as a reform journalist. In 1893, a different issue concerning gold calls for Henry's attention. This time, the question is whether international trade should be based exclusively on payment of balances in gold or on a combination of gold and silver. Adams supports the silver backers—primarily small businessmen, laborers, debtors, and farmers—because he is wary of the control of bankers and other gold capitalists, whom Henry calls *gold-bugs*.

After a visit to Cuba with Clarence King in 1894, Henry becomes devoted to the cause of Cuban independence from Spain, proposing to Congress a peaceful, diplomatic resolution titled "Recognition of Cuban Independence" (December 21, 1896). Because diplomacy fails, Adams welcomes the Spanish-American War of 1898, which results in Cuban independence.

Henry's interest in the Christian unity of the Middle Ages is part of one of the most important dichotomies in his character. Adams has gained an appreciation for the significance of the Church and its symbols—the Virgin, the mass, the cathedral—in the lives of fourteenth-century Christians. The Church is a unifying force, and Henry admires the comfort and direction that the people share. Near the end of 1900 or the beginning of 1901, he composes a poem titled "Prayer to the Virgin of Chartres." The poem expresses the theme and recognizes the force of medieval Christianity as expressed in the miracles attributed to the Virgin as well as in belief of the Madonna's capacity to intervene on behalf of her people through prayer. Having studied Gothic architecture intensely since 1895, Henry also writes his *Mont-Saint-Michel and Chartres*, a historical and philosophical meditation on medieval unity, which is published in 1904.

In contrast, the last third of the *Education* is increasingly concerned with the scientific multiplicity of the modern era. Expositions in Chicago, Paris, and St. Louis attract Henry's attention to a new direction for mankind. The comfortable unity of the Middle Ages has been replaced by scientific multiplicity. There are no longer any simple answers. People must struggle to maintain control over scientific advance. Henry believes that mankind will need to make a dramatic increase in intellect just to deal with all of the scientific data arriving in the twentieth century. Part of his "Prayer to the Virgin of Chartres" (1900–1901) is a section titled "Prayer to the Dynamo"; in it, mankind has lost its innocence along with its unifying faith and finds itself in a materialistic world, worshipping the dynamo. Technology has replaced the Church. Adams does not necessarily prefer this. In fact, he seems nostalgic for the simple unity of the Middle Ages. But as a historian and an intellect, he must recognize what is happening and try to incorporate scientific thought into his own approach to history. This is the starting point of the closing chapters of the book in which he does develop a "Dynamic Theory of History" (1904). As a companion piece to the *Chartres*, Adams writes *The Education of Henry Adams* (1907), a study in multiplicity.

Within the context of an experimental work of literature, Adams makes effective use of symbol and theme. The result is a hybrid of biography, history, fiction, and philosophy, which Modern Library calls the best work of nonfiction in English in the twentieth century.

CliffsNotes Review

Use this CliffsNotes Review to test your understanding of the original text and reinforce what you've learned in this book. After you work through the review and essay questions and the fun and useful practice projects, you're well on your way to understanding a comprehensive and meaningful interpretation of *The Education of Henry Adams*.

Q&A

1. As a boy, Henry spends summers in

    a) Boston

    b) The Catskills

    c) Quincy

    d) Vermont

2. As a senior at Harvard, Henry is named

    a) Valedictorian

    b) Salutatorian

    c) Top Math Student

    d) Class Orator

3. In Berlin, Adams spends most of his class time studying

    a) German at a prep school

    b) Cooking at the *Küchenchef*

    c) Writing at the *Urheber*

    d) History at the University of Berlin

4. Henry's sister Louisa dies as the result of

    a) Childbirth

    b) Malaria

    c) Ennui

    d) Tetanus

5. Henry meets Clarence King at

    a) John Hay's wedding

    b) a geological convention

    c) Estes Park

    d) Louisa's bat mitzvah

6. The leader of the slum gang in the infamous snowball fight is _____.

7. Henry's next-door adult friend in Washington, eventually Secretary of State, is _____.

8. The woman who becomes Henry's emotional confidante after Marian's suicide is _____.

9. _____ is the companion piece for *The Education of Henry Adams*.

10. Henry spends most of the American Civil War in London serving as _____.

Answers: (1) c. (2) d. (3) a. (4) d. (5) c. (6) Conky Daniels. (7) John Hay. (8) Elizabeth Cameron. (9) *Mont-Saint-Michel and Chartres*. (10) His father's private secretary.

Identify the Quote

1. "The actual journey may have been quite different, but the actual journey has no interest for education."

2. "Probably no child, born in the year, held better cards than he."

3. "No man can instruct more than half a dozen students at once."

4. "Venice would be a fine city if it were drained."

5. "Every friend in power is a friend lost."

6. "A teacher affects eternity; he can never tell where his influence stops."

7. "Let us have peace."

8. "The English mind was one-sided, eccentric, systematically unsystematic and logically illogical."

9. "Gold-bugs."

10. "He was an acrobat, with a dwarf on his back, crossing a chasm on a slack-rope, and commonly breaking his neck."

Answers: 1) The narrator speaking of Henry's trip to Washington, D. C., in 1850. 2) The narrator speaks of Henry's privileged birth in 1838. 3) Adams's theory of class size, expressed in relationship to Harvard. 4) Ulysses S. Grant's observation regarding international attractions. 5) Henry's conclusion, specifically prompted by Secretary of State Seward. 6) One of Henry's best known aphorisms, concerning Harvard. 7) Grant accepting nomination for presidency, May 29, 1868; Henry sees a second meaning: that Grant wants to be left alone. 8) Representative of Henry's bias against the English and his love for paradox, regarding his time in London (1863). 9) Henry's term for gold capitalists during gold-silver conflict of 1890s. 10) Henry invents this metaphor while considering man's position in the universe as part of the "Abyss of Ignorance" (Chapter XXIX).

Essay Questions

1. The author sometimes associates a major symbol with a major theme. Choose one of each and demonstrate how he uses the symbol to illustrate the theme.

2. Henry spends important formative years in England as his father's personal secretary. What does he learn? How, if at all, does he change during this period?

3. Discuss Henry's attitude toward formal education. What are his complaints about it, and what solutions does he offer?

4. Describe Henry's experience in Germany during the "Grand Tour" following his graduation from Harvard. Consider his involvement with education, the arts, food and drink, and the culture generally.

5. The death of Henry's sister Louisa is a profound event in his life. How does he present this to the reader? What is his reaction to the tragedy? What seems to bring him back to the living?

6. What are the major historical eras in Adams's "Dynamic Theory of History"? Define what he means by "force" and briefly describe what Adams sees as the central force of each era.

7. What does Henry see during his trip to Maryland, Virginia and Washington, D. C., in 1850? As a twelve-year-old boy, how does he react to these experiences?

8. What do you think the narrator means by "education"? Considering his point of view, what do you see as the most "educational" experience in the book?

9. How important is the twenty-year gap in the story? If you had been Adams, would you have left out the events of those years? Does it bother you that he did? Why or why not?

10. What is the *Pteraspis*? How does the author use it to enrich or enliven the story?

Practice Projects

1. Choose a recent event in your life or in your community and write a one-page description of it, in the style of Henry Adams.

2. You are an investigative reporter for the New York *Times* from 1860 to 1905. Which of the stories that Adams discusses would you prefer to cover? Whom would you interview? What questions would you ask? What other approaches would you use?

3. Most of the *Education* is in narrative form. As a class project, divide into groups, each group choosing an event to dramatize. Assign individuals to play actual people and create a scene or two, with dialogue, that may have occurred.

4. What do you think has been the most "educational" event in your own life? Describe it in your own words, telling the reader what you mean by "educational" and why you choose this event.

5. The Internet has relatively little to say about Henry Adams or this book. Working together, have the class design its own Web site for the *Education* and decide what will be featured on the various pages.

CliffsNotes Resource Center

The learning doesn't need to stop here. CliffsNotes Resource Center shows you the best of the best links to the best information in print and online about the author and/or related works. And don't think that this is all we've prepared for you; we've put all kinds of pertinent information at www.cliffsnotes.com. Look for all the terrific resources at your favorite bookstore or local library and on the Internet. When you're online, make your first stop www.cliffsnotes.com where you'll find more incredibly useful information about Henry Adams and *The Education of Henry Adams*.

Books

This CliffsNotes book, published by IDG Books Worldwide, Inc., provides a meaningful interpretation of *The Education of Henry Adams*. If you are looking for information about the author and/or related works, check out these other publications:

Bishop, Ferman. *Henry Adams*. Boston: Twayne Publishers, 1979. Students assigned to write research papers will find the extensive annotated bibliography useful. The text is especially strong on background information and commentary regarding Adams's major works.

Gooder, Jean, ed. *The Education of Henry Adams*. New York: Penguin Putnam Inc., 1995. This edition features informative notes, a brief bibliography, a reliable chronology, and a worthwhile introduction by Gooder. Highly recommended.

Harbert, Earl N. *Critical Essays on Henry Adams*. Boston: G. K. Hall & Co., 1981. An excellent collection of some of the most important critical commentary up to 1981, including essays by Ernest Samuels and J. C. Levenson.

O'Toole, Patricia. *The Five of Hearts: An Intimate Portrait of Henry Adams & His Friends, 1880–1918*. New York: C. N. Potter, 1990. Adams's intimate circle of friends contributed to his work as well as his personal well-being. This is an excellent study of the symbiosis of friendship and creative energy.

Rowe, John Carlos, ed. *New Essays on The Education of Henry Adams*. New York: Cambridge University Press, 1996. The strength of the work is placing the *Education* in its historic context, but there is an insightful article by Martha Banta on Adams's personal nature.

Samuels, Ernest. *The Young Henry Adams*. Cambridge, Massachusetts: Harvard University Press, 1948. *Henry Adams: The Middle Years*. Cambridge, Massachusetts: Harvard University Press, 1958. *Henry Adams: The Major Phase*. Cambridge, Massachusetts: Harvard University Press, 1964. In these three volumes, Samuels presents the definitive critical biography of Henry Adams, works that any serious scholar must consult repeatedly. Highly recommended.

J. C. Levenson, Ernest Samuels, Charles Vandersee and Viola Hopkins Winner, editors. *The Letters of Henry Adams* (six volumes). Cambridge, Massachusetts: Harvard University Press, 1982-88. This is a treasure. Adams's letters are informative and entertaining, and students can check Adams's private comments about events on a certain date. Samuels has also edited a single-volume *Selected Letters* (1992), which is more convenient for most students and includes several interesting photographs.

Simpson, Brooks. *The Political Education of Henry Adams*. Columbia, S. C.: University of South Carolina Press, 1996. Simpson effectively traces Adams's metamorphosis from political neophyte to sage. Very worthwhile.

It's easy to find books published by IDG Books Worldwide, Inc. and other publishers. You'll find them in your favorite bookstores (on the Internet and at a store near you). IDG Books also has three Web sites that you can use to read about all the books we publish:

- www.cliffsnotes.com
- www.dummies.com
- www.idgbooks.com

Internet

Abraham Lincoln: An Educational Site, www.geocities.com/Sunset Strip/Venue/5217/lincoln.html—Enlightening and colorful with detailed information, lots of photographs, and some letters. Novices and experts alike should find this site fascinating.

Adams National Historic Site, www.nps.gov/adam—Offers a visit to location of Adams's boyhood home and includes worthwhile photographs.

Amazon.com, www.amazon.com—The site offers reviews of books by customers, which are often of interest, as well as comments by scholars and professional critics.

The Boxer Rebellion, www.smplanet.com/imperialism/fists.html—Features links to maps of China and John Hay's first "Open Door" note, as well as a discussion of the rebellion, its causes, and its resolution.

The Civil War Home Page, www.civil-war.net/main.html—A wealth of wonderful information including battle summaries, photographs, audio and printed lyrics of music of the day, diaries, and much more.

Grave of Henry Adams, www.findagrave.com—Interesting photograph of the graves of Henry and Marian with the Augustus Saint-Gaudens sculpture at Rock Creek Cemetery in Washington, D. C.

Massachusetts Historical Society, www.masshist.org—A collection of the Adams papers and books from his personal library.

Modern Library 100 Best Nonfiction, www.randomhouse.com/modernlibrary/100best/list.html—The *Education* tops the list of best nonfiction books in English in the twentieth century, but the other ninety-nine are also of interest.

Ulysses S. Grant Home Page, www.mscomm.com/~ulysses/(Public and personal information including personality, favorite books, interviews, drinking habits, diaries, doodles, and letters. Especially informative regarding the private side of the man.

Next time you're on the Internet, don't forget to drop by www.cliffsnotes.com. We've created an online Resource Center that you can use today, tomorrow, and beyond.

Articles

Adams, Brooks. "The Heritage of Henry Adams." *The Degradation of the Democratic Dogma.* New York: Macmillan, 1919. Worthwhile for historical purposes, the essay suggests that Henry is the philosophical, as well as biological, descendant of John Quincy Adams.

Eliot, T. S. "A Skeptical Patrician." *The Athenaeum* (23 May 1919), 361–362. This early recognition, by the renowned poet and critic, helped set the tone for further scholarship.

Colacurcio, Michael. "The Dynamo and the Angelic Doctor: The Bias of Henry Adams' Medievalism." *American Quarterly* 17 (1965), 696–712. Representative of the controversy often surrounding Adams criticism, this article makes an interesting argument that Adams found modern chaos in medieval philosophy, especially that of Thomas Aquinas.

Index

A

accidental education, 29
Adams, Abigail, 2
Adams, Charles Francis, 2, 11, 20, 31
  character analysis of, 98, 99
  diplomatic successes in Britain, 36, 38,
    40, 41, 99, 106
Adams, Charles Francis, Jr., 13, 29, 30, 55
Adams, Charles Kendall, 60
Adams, Henry
  as Harvard professor, 3, 12, 59
  as London correspondent for New York
    Times, 33, 34
  as political journalist, 95
  as private secretary to father, 31
  as Washington correspondent for Boston
    Daily Advertiser, 31, 32
  background of, 2–4
  bankers, distrust of, 63
  childhood of, 10, 18
  constructionist beliefs, 50, 54
  correspondence with Charles, 29, 30
  death of, 4, 90
  devotion to correspondence, 67
  disciplining by John Quincy, 18, 19
  educational innovations, 3, 12
  formal education of, 2
  fortuitous position of, 49, 94
  friends of, 4
  German language, inadequacy with, 27
  income of, 49
  Indian summer, 66
  intellectual curiosity, 94, 97
  law studies, 29, 31
  life of privilege, questioning of, 22
  love for teaching and students, 59
  Marian's suicide, effect on, 3
  marriage of, 3, 59
  mathematics, weakness in, 26
  objective treatment, 11
  public personality, 50
  published works of, 4–6, 60
  Pulitzer Prize, 4
  reformist career, 53
  return to States, 49

  reviews of, 52
  scarlet fever, 18, 19
  social disdain of, 43
  travels of, 62, 104
  verbal skills, 26, 50
  writing career, 2, 3, 11, 32, 46, 52, 53
  writing, skill in, 26
Adams, John, 2
Adams, John Quincy, 2, 10
  stroke of, 18, 19
Alabama, 37, 41
American Ministry in England, 45
Antiquity of Man (Lyell), 47
Aquinas, Thomas, 70, 79
art, Henry's interest in, 46

B

Bacon, Francis, 88
battering rams, 40
beliefs, replacement of, 10
Berlin, 2, 11, 27, 28, 95, 103
Bishop, Ferman, 6
Black Friday, 54
Booth, John Wilkes, 45
Boston, 18
  young Henry's perception of, 18
Boutwell, George S., 52
Boxer Rebellion, 72
Britain
  diplomatic recognition of
    Confederacy, 36
  financial interests in Confederacy, 37
  neutrality during Civil War, 11, 33, 37,
    38, 99, 106
  support for Confederacy, 33, 36, 38, 40
Brooks, Peter Chardon, 22
Butler, Benjamin Franklin, 36

C

Cameron, Elizabeth, 4, 62, 69, 70
Cameron, James Donald, 62, 65, 70
capitalist system, 65
Carlyle, Thomas, 10
characters, list of, 12, 14
checks and balances, 55
China, open doors of, 80, 85
Christianity, medieval, 6, 12, 69, 70, 104
  unity in, 73
civil service reform, 53

Germany, 27, 28
    relationship with England and France,
        75, 81
Gladstone, William Ewert, 38
Gold Scandal of September 1869, 54, 55
gold standard, 4, 52, 64, 96
gold, drop in value, 54
gold-bugs, 65
Gooder, Jean, 50, 85
Gould, Jay, 54
Grammar of Science, The (Pearson), 83
Grand Tour of Europe, 11, 27, 29
Grant, Ulysses S., 49
    Henry's disappointment in, 52, 53
Gray, Horace A., 31
great secession winter, 31
greenback currency, 50, 52

H

Hale, Charles, 32
Harvard University
    Henry's criticism of, 2, 25
    Henry's professorship, 3, 12, 58, 59, 60,
        62, 95
Hay, John, 4, 62, 64, 67, 72, 73, 80, 85, 90
    character analysis of, 97, 98
Hearst, William Randolph, 67
Hegel, 73
Henry. See also Adams, Henry
    character of, 12
Henry Adams: The Middle Years (Samuels),
    5, 62
history
    graduate studies in, 3
    scientific study of, 4, 48
    theory of, 76, 78
History of the United States of America
    during the Administrations of Thomas
    Jefferson and James Madison (Adams), 3,
    5, 62
Hooper, Marian, 3, 12, 62
House of Baring, 62, 64

I

idealism, 26
ignorance, abyss of, 10, 76
illness, 19
inertia, of political influence, 80, 81
innocence, loss of, 105
international politics, 80, 81, 85

international trade, 64
island life, 104
Italy, Henry's stay in, 45

J

James, William, 8
John Randolph (Adams), 3, 5
Johnson, Andrew, 45
joy, education of, 19

K

King, Clarence, 4, 12, 60, 62, 64, 66, 67,
    75, 90
    character analysis of, 99, 100
Kuhn, Charles, 29
Kuhn, Louisa Catherine (Adams), 3, 12, 29
    death of, 57

L

La Farge, John, 4, 62
laissez-faire, 52, 55
leap of intellect, 88, 89
lecture system, 95
Lee, Robert E., 38
Legal Tender Act, 50, 54, 55
Letters of Henry Adams, The (Samuels), 62
Life of Albert Gallatin, The (Adams), 3
Lincoln, Abraham, 31, 45
    Henry's impression of, 45
lines of force, 78
Lodge, Henry Cabot, 8
London
    diplomatic strain in, 33–38, 40–42
    Henry's criticism of, 34, 42, 43, 103
    Henry's vacation in, 57
    social scene, 35, 42
Lyell, Charles, 47, 48, 104

M

Maine, 67
Major Phase, The (Samuels), 87
manikin persona, 9, 11, 18, 102
mathematics, 21
Memoirs of Marau Taaroa, Last Queen of
    Tahiti (Adams), 104
Mont-Saint-Michel and Chartres (Adams), 4,
    6, 78, 79, 90
Moran, Benjamin, 43

NOTES